Anonymus

A daily exercise and devotions

For the young ladies and gentlewomen pensioners

Anonymus

A daily exercise and devotions
For the young ladies and gentlewomen pensioners

ISBN/EAN: 9783741166341

Manufactured in Europe, USA, Canada, Australia, Japa

Cover: Foto ©Thomas Meinert / pixelio.de

Manufactured and distributed by brebook publishing software
(www.brebook.com)

Anonymus

A daily exercise and devotions

A
DAILY EXERCISE,
AND
DEVOTIONS,
FOR
THE YOUNG LADIES,
AND GENTLEWOMEN
PENSIONERS
*At the Monaſtery of the English
Canoneſſes Regulars of the
Holy Order of*

S. AUGUSTIN,
AT BRUGES.

Collected from many good Authors.

AT BRUGES,
Printed with permiſſion by C. DE MOOR,
in the Name JESU.

M. DCC. LXXXVI.

TO THE
QUEEN OF HEAVEN.

WIth all imaginable refpect, O Queen of heaven and earth, we offer you this little work, compos'd of divers Prayers and Devotions which regard the honour of your Son, and glory of his name; which makes us hope you will take it under your protection, and obtain his facred benedictions on the young fouls, for whofe ufe it is publis'd. O moft pure Virgin obtain for them of your divine Son graces neceffary to fructifie this Holy feed in the bottom of their hearts, to the end that having prais'd and lov'd him upon earth, they may continue the fame for à whole eternity in heaven. Amen.

A DAILY EXERCISE

AND

PRAYERS FOR THE

PENSIONERS

AT THE

AUGUSTIN NUNNS AT BRUGES.

As foon as you are call'd endeavour to awake to God : Both your good Angel, and the devil are watching for your firft thoughts and words, which the one would offer to God, the other fteal from him ; fay, Behold me O Lord becaufe you have call'd me. *Then* in the name of the Father &c. *and figning your felf with the fign of the Crofs. Say* Jesus I give you my heart, my actions, and my thoughts.

After that, readily and modeftly put on your cloaths, as call'd upon by our bleffed Lord to adore him, therefore refolve not to fpeak to any creature till you have done fo.

In putting on your peticoat say.

O Sweet JESUS, by your moſt Humble poverty, I beg the garment of humility.

In putting on your night gown.

DEar Lord I moſt humbly beſeech you for
the love of your ſelf, and of your moſt Bleſſed
Mother, to beſtow upon me the robe of purity.

*As ſoon as decently you can, kneel down to
adore our Lord, begging his and our Ladies
bleſsing, and giving thanks to God for having
preſerv'd you that night, and given you another day to ſerve him in, and work your ſalvation ; for which you may uſe theſe or the
like forms.*

Proſtrate moſt humbly at the feet of your
Souverain and Divine Majeſty, I adore, bleſs,
and glorifie you, O moſt Holy Trinity, Almighty God, Father, Son, and Holy Ghoſt;
I praiſe, and thank you with all the affections
of my heart for all the benefits I have receiv'd
from your pure goodneſs, and mercy; particularly for that you have been pleas'd to pre-
ſerve me this night, and give me this day to
encreaſe in your Holy fear and love ; grant I
may employ it all to your glory, and never
mortally offend you. Amen.

A Prayer to the Bleſſed Virgin.

O Holy Virgin, moſt powerful Queen of heaven and earth, and my dear Advocatreſs, I

falute you by the moſt aimable heart of your Son JESUS, moſt humbly beſeeching you to aſſiſt me in all my ſpiritual, and corporal ne-ceſſities, and eſpecially at the hour of my death. Amen.

In combing your head.

GRant I m... humbly beſeech you, O my God, that my thoughts, which are the hairs of my ſoul, may be ſo well cleans'd and pu-rify'd by your Holy fear, that they may never diſpleaſe you. Amen.

In dreſsing your head.

I Dreſs and adorn my head, O my Saviour, and yours was crown'd with thorns : ah ! wound my heart with the thorn of à true con-trition, and let all my thoughts have no other end but you. Amen.

My God I moſt humbly beſeech you to give me the virtue of modeſty ; and ſince à young Damſel cannot forget the fineſt of her ornaments, permit me not my God ever to forget you, who art the moſt precious orna-ment of my ſoul. Amen.

In putting on your mantow.

MY God I moſt humbly beſeech you to cloath me with the robe of charity. Amen.

In washing your hands.

MAy the blood and water which iſſu'd from your ſacred ſide, O dear JESUS, waſh away the filth of my ſoul. Amen.

*Being quite dreft, attend to the morning
Prayers, and fay them in your heart, or if
you can, repeat them after the officiant, they
are as follows.*

Bleffed be the moft Holy and undivided
Trinity, Father, Son, and Holy Ghoft, now
and for ever, world without end. Amen.
Then our Father, and Hail Mary &c.
I Believe in God, &c.
℣. Vouchfafe O Lord to keep us this day.
℞. Without fin.
℣. Have mercy on us O Lord.
℞. Have mercy on us.
℣. Thy mercy be upon us, O Lord.
℞. As we have put our truft in thee,
℣. O Lord hear our Prayer.
℞. And let our fupplication come unto thee.

Let us Pray.

LOrd God omnipotent, Who haft brought
us to the beginning of this day, vouchfafe
to preferve us by your power, that this day
we fall not into any fin, but that your juftice
accompany all our thoughts, words, and
works, through JESUS CHRIST our Lord. &c.

Lord God, King of heaven and earth,
vouchfafe to conduct, fanctifie, and govern
this day, our bodies, fenfes, difcourfes, and
actions, to the end that in the courfe of this
life, and in the eternity of the future, we may

be fav'd by the help of your Holy grace; who
liveft and raigneft world without end. Amen.

O Angels of God to whofe Holy care we are
committed by the fupreme clemency, illuminate, defend, and govern us this day, in all
our thoughts, words, and Actions. Amen.

Blefs us O Lord, and preferve us from all
evil, and bring us to eternall life : and may
the fouls of the Faithfull Departed thro' the
mercy of God reft in peace. Amen.

*Acts of Adoration, thanksgiving and
Offering.*

ALmighty and everlafting God, in union
of the great purity, moft profound humility,
ardent charity, love, ad reverence with which
all the elect, both in heaven and on earth
have, and do adore, love, and ferve you,
offering themfelves continually to you ; we
adore you, love you, and render you millions
of thanks for all the benefits we have ever
receiv'd of your infinit goodnefs; particularly
that it hath pleas'd you to create us to your
image and likenefs, and preferve us till this
prefent; for having fav'd us and redeem'd us
with the price of your moft Precious Blood,
induring fo great pains and torments for us ;
for having call'd us to the Holy Catholick
Faith and Religion, as alfo for having juftify'd
us in pardoning us our fins. Infine, my God,

we moſt humbly thank you for having preſerv'd us this night from ſudden death, and
from all the dangers and ſins into which we
had fall'n, if we had not been ſuſtain'd by
your powerful and merciful hand. Alas, my
God, what return ſhall we make for ſo many
favours? We who are nothing, have nothing,
and can do nothing; at leaſt we conſecrate
offer, and dedicate to you, our bodies with
all their ſenſes, our ſouls with all their powers,
our hearts with all their deſires, all our
thoughts, words, actions, motions, and reſ-
pirations; profeſſing, that with the aſſiſtance
of your Holy grace, we will neither think,
ſpeak, nor do any thing this day nor hereafter,
but for the greater glory and praiſe of your
moſt Holy name. Amen.

A Prayer to our Lady.

O Holy Virgin, Mother of God, Queen of
Angels and Men, we ſalute and reverence you
with all our hearts, as your moſt Bleſſed Son
would have you be honour'd in heaven and
upon earth, O Mother of mercy, we this day
chuſe you for our Mother; regard us as yours,
and by your goodneſs, treat us as the objects
of your mercy : Mother of goodneſs and refuge
of ſinners, we make recourſe to you to be deliver'd from eternal death, take us into your
protection.

Give us your Holy benediction : may we be

of the number of your faithfull servants, and
may the last hour of our lives be in your hands.
Amen.

*May the Virgin Mary obtain us the bles-
sing of her divine Son.*

Come Holy Ghost, replenish the hearts of the
faithfull; and kindle in them the fire of thy love.

*Observe due recollection in going to Mass,
or you will have but little devotion in time of it:
beg our Lady as you go along, to obtain you
the dispositions the mystery requires, saying.*

O Queen of heaven and earth, obtain for
me by your powerful intercession, the grace
to hear this mass with attention, devotion,
and tenderness of love, answerable to those
you had in going towards Mount Calvary,
when in a bloody and visible way, the same
sacrifice was there to be offer'd for the redemption of all mankind. Amen.

In taking Holy-water.

SPrinkle me O Lord with hysop and I shall
be cleans'd : wash me, and I shall be made
whiter than snow.

*Entering into the Quire, remember you enter
into the King of heavens presence-chamber :
and being kneel'd down in your place, make
the sign of the cross, and adore Divine JE-
SUS with a low bow, Saying.*

Almighty and Everlasting God, who art here
present to receive the homages and adorations

of your creatures; and who refides in the moft
Blefled Sacrament of the Altar, to replenish us
with your favours and graces; I adore you with
all my heart; and moft humbly, and inftantly
befeech you, to grant me the grace, to com-
port my felf, before your Divine Majefty with
all due devotion and refpect. Amen.

*Remember to make your intention for the
enfuing Mafs, to which you may add thefe
following Prayers.*

On Sunday.

MOft Holy and Adorable Trinity, t' is to
honour and glorific you, that I hear this
Mafs, and to obtain of your infinite goodnefs
the converfion of pagans and infidels.

On Munday.

I Offer you, O Holy Ghoft, this divine Sacrifice of the Mafs for your honour and glory,
and to obtain of your infinite goodnefs, lights.
and efficacious graces to know, and accomplish perfectly your holy will. I alfo offer it for
the repofe of the fouls in purgatory, and particularly for that foul that is fooneft to enjoy
you in heaven.

On Tuesday.

I Offer you, O my God, the Holy Sacrifice of
the Mafs, to render you moft humble thanks

for the favours you have done to the glorious
Saint Michaël, and all the Holy Angels. I alſo
offer it in thanksgiving for my Angel Guardian,
and to obtain of your infinit goodneſs, the grace
to be moſt devout and obedient to him.

On Wednesday.

I Offer you, my God, the Holy Sacrifice of the
Maſs, in thanksgiving for all the benefits both
general and particular, that I have receiv'd
from your liberal goodneſs. I offer it alſo in
thanksgiving for thoſe you have beſtow'd upon
all the Saints in heaven, and in particular for
the favours you have granted to the glorious
St. Joſeph, and to my Patrons and Patroneſ-
ſes; and to obtain the grace of following, and
imitating their holy examples.

On Thursday.

I Offer you, O my God, the Holy Sacrifice of
the Maſs, to render you millions of thanks for
the ſeven Sacraments, eſpecially the moſt Blef-
ſed Sacrament of the Altar, that Divine food
of our ſouls, and to obtain of your infinite
goodneſs the grace never to receive it unworthily, and at my death to receive it by
way of Viaticum, together with the other requiſite Sacraments.

ON FRYDAY.

I Offer you, my God, the Holy Sacrifice of the Mafs, in thanksgiving for the infinite benefit of your death and paffion; and by it I conjure you efficaciously to apply the merits thereof, to me and all poor finners, that we may never be feparated from you.

ON SATURDAY.

I Offer you, O my God, the Holy Sacrifice of the Mafs, to thank you moft cordially for having chofen the Blefled Virgin to be your Mother, and for all the other graces, and prerogatives that you have beftow'd upon her: and to obtain the grace of loving, honouring, ferving, and imitating her all the days of my life. And you, O moft holy Mother of God, I conjure you to take me into your protection; and as Mother of mercy, to obtain for me of your divine Son, the pardon of all my fins, the grace of à happy death, and that I may never be feparated from him.

UPON HOLY DAYS ADD.

I Offer it alfo to fatisfie my obligation, and in honour of fuch à Saint, N. N.

At the beginning of the Mafs make the fign of the Crofs again, and remembring that you are all that time actually adoring God prefent, never fit at à low Mafs, if you are well, much less neglect Gods presence so far, as to look about, or lean, or make any unnecessary noise.

Say, the Confiteor *with the Priest, producing Acts of Contrition.*

At the Gospel rise, and with your thumb make the sign of the Cross upon your forehead, mouth, and breast, then recite the Creed *making Acts of Faith.*

In time of Mass say the hours of our Ladies office, or if you have them not, the Prayers in your manuel according to the day of the week.

Considering some Miftery of your Saviours life, and Pafsion.

After Sanctus *Offer the Sacrifice to God, saying.*

O Infinite Majefty, receive and accept this Holy Sacrifice, which is offer'd you by your Son, and the whole Church, for an eternal praife, in acknowledgment of, and homage to the foverain dominion you have over me, and all creatures : I offer it you alfo, O my God, in thanksgiving for all your benefits; receive it alfo I befeech you, in fatisfaction for my fins, and for thofe of the living and faithful departed; and to obtain the bleffings, both fpiritual and temporal, which are neceffary for the good of your Church, and the falvation of our fouls. Amen.

A little before the Confecration pull of your

*gloves; and at the Elevation of the Holy Hoft,
fay devoutly with your hands join'd.*

O Saving Hoft which heaven's gate laidft open
at fo dear a rate by Hoftile wars we are oppreft
be thou our aid fupport & reft.

At the Elevation of the Chalice.

Hail moft precious & facred Blood, which
flowing out of the fide of my Lord & faviour
JESUS CHRIST, wafheft away the fpots of our
offences; cleanfe, fanctify, & preferve my foul,
I befeech thee, to everlafting life.

After the Elevation fay.

O Father of infinit mercy, I moft humbly
befeech you by the Precious Blood of your
Son, which was fhed upon the Crofs with fo
many amorous pains, and which has now been
offer'd you on this Altar, to enlighten the
whole world, preferve the Holy Church, our
Holy Father the Pope, the Cardinals, Arch-
bishops, Bishops, Preachers, and generally
all thofe that are oblig'd to the conduct of
fouls. And as you are the King of Kings,
by whom alone all Kings reign and command,
I befeech you to govern and protect our
King, Queen, Prince, and Princeffes, as alfo
my Father, and Mother, Parents, Friends,
and Benefactors; and to grant mercy to my
enemies, pardon to all finners, peace to the
living, and eternal reft to the faithful departed

Infine my God I moſt humbly beg pardon
for my ſins, and the grace ſo to renounce my
ſelf, that my will may perfectly be transform'd
into yours. Amen.

At the Prieſts Communion ſay three times.

LOrd, I am not worthy that thoushould'ſt
enter under my roof, ſay only the word, and
my ſoul ſhall be heal'd.

Then communicate ſpiritually ſaying.

O ſweet JESUS, I moſt ardently deſire
you, my heart ſighs after you : Celeſtial bread,
I deſire to receive you with humility and due
reverence; but knowing my ſelf unworthy to
approach this Divine Sacrament, I moſt humbly beſeech you, at leaſt, to enter ſpiritually
into my ſoul. Come then, O JESUS! Come,
O Divine Food! Come, O ſweetneſs of my
ſoul! Come enrich me with your graces : give
your ſelf to me Lord, and by your mercy
grant I may be alſo wholy yours. Amen.

*When the Prieſt gives the Benediction,
receive it devoutly, begging of God, à bleſſing for all the enſuing day. Before you
leave the Quire adore our Lord, ſaying.*

We adore thee O Chriſte, & bleſs thee, becauſe by thy holy Croſs thou haſt redeemed the
world :

world : Lord who died for us have mercy on us.

After Mafs, thofe that are capable of it, remain in the Quire à quarter of an hour to keep their meditation, in order to which there is à method p. 85.

Then make the fign of the Crofs, and after you are rifen , make à profund reverence to the Bleffed Sacrament.

At the Quire door take Holy-water , as at your entrance, and obferve what has been faid for coming in , and going out of the Quire every time you do fo.

In returning to the fchool, thank God for the blefsings receiv'd at Mafs, to which end you may fay the Te Deum, *foftly.*

When it rings to work, you fay the Salve Regina, *and Prayer, with this following.*

I Offer you , O my God, the work I am going about for your honour and glory, and purely for the love of you ; in union of the Holy works and actions, that your moft dear Son, our Lord and Saviour JESUS-CHRIST did, being in this world : I moft humbly befeech you to illuminate me, guide me, and conduct me in this, fo that I may therein pleafe you , and accomplish your moft holy will. Amen. ·

B

Before you begin to learn any thing,
say softly.

O Eternel Wisdom, enlighten my understanding, and strengthen my memory, that I
may well comprehend what I am going to
learn to your greater glory. Amen.

When you find à difficulty in doing any
thing, say.

I Will for the love of you, O my God, acquit my self of this duty, notwithstanding the
repugnance I find in it.

Let diligence and constancy equally accom-
pany your work, and piety always season it
by frequent aspirations, elevating your heart
to God. Saying.

My God grant me the grace to love you
sincerely.

Or the like, page the 141. wishing each
stitch might produce an act of love, which
may render your work as meritorious as
Prayer.

In saying your Beads, reflect on the mys-
teries of our Saviours life, and passion &c
And let modesty, Zeal, devotion, tendernes
of affections, and attention, sanctifie that
action.

For the examen before dinner the officiant
says aloud, and the reft the three
Acts softly.

WE muft remember that God who is every
where, is here prefent; and that he is the
abfolute mafter of our lives : let us then give
him à faithfull account of this morning ; and
for the firft point, let us begin by thanksgiving for the benefits we have receiv'd from
his liberal hand.

ACT OF THANKSGIVING.

I Adore you, O my God, I praife and thank
you, my Soverain Lord, and moft liberal
benefactor; I invite all creatures to praife and
thank you with me, for all the benefits both
of nature and grace, common and particular,
which I have receiv'd of your infinite mercy
and liberality; and principally for having preferv'd me this day, affifted me with your Holy
grace, and preferv'd me by à particular protection from many evils, both fpiritual and
corporal which otherwife might have happen'd
to me.

For the fecond point, let us beg the
affiftance of the Holy Ghoft for to
know our faults.

ACT OF A MOST HUMBLE PETITION.

O My God, fince I moft ungratefull creature, after fo many benefits ceafe not to fall

every hour into fin, I moft humbly befeech
you to open the eyes of my foul, that I may
know my faults, to beg pardon, and do penance for them. Come Holy Ghoft, replenish
the hearts of the faithfull, and kindle in them
the fire of thy love.

*For the third point, let us examen the faults
we have committed, by thoughts, words,
works, and omifsions, in particular thofe
whereto we find our felves moft inclin'd.*

*Here make the examen, which being ended,
the Officiant goes on.*

*For the fourth and fifth point, let us
ask pardon of God, and purpofe to
do better hereafter.*

ACT OF CONTRITION.

O Lord JESUS-CHRIST, true God and true
Man, my Creator and Redeemer. I am forry
with all my heart for having offended you,
and this for the love of your felf, who art
an infinit goodnefs, worthy to be lov'd above
all things. I purpofe firmly, by the affiftance
of your Holy grace, never to offend you
more, to amend my life, to withdraw my
felf from all occafions of fin, to confefs them
entirely, and to do the penance which shall
be enjoyn'd me.

GRACE BEFORE MEALS AT DINNER.

Bless us O Lord, and thefe thy gifts, which of thy bounty we are going to receive thro CHRIST our Lord. Amen. May the King of eternal glory make us participate of his Heavenly banquet. Amen.

AT SUPPER.

Blefs us O Lord, and thefe thy gifts, which of thy bounty we are going to receive thro CHRIST our Lord. Amen. May the King of eternal glory, conduct us to the Supper of eternal life. Amen.

GRACE AFTER DINNER AND SUPPER.

But thou O Lord, have mercy on us. R. Thanks be to God.

We give thee thanks almighty God, for all thy benefits, thrò JESUS CHRIST our Lord. Amen. Lord have mercy on us, CHRIST have mercy on us, Lord have mercy on us. Our Father &c. And lead us not into temptation but deliver us fom evil. Amen.

℣. The name of our Lord be to bleffed.

℟. From henceforth now and for ever.

Vouchfafe O Lord, for thy name fake to render eternal life to all thefe that do us good. Amen.

℣. Blefs us O Lord.

℟. Thanks be to God.

And. May the fouls of the faithful thrô the mercy of God reſt in peace. Amen. Our Father in ſecret. May God give us his Peace. Amen.

At Veſpers you go again to the Quire, and whenever you do ſo, obſerve what has been already ſaid both for the coming in, and going out.

In time of Veſpers, ſay Veſpers and Complin, the Matins and Lauds of our Ladies Office for the next day: or (if you do not ſay it) the evening Prayers for the day, which you have in your manual. Conclude with this Prayer to S. Joſeph.

A PRAYER TO S. JOSEPH.

O Moſt powerful Saint, foſter Father to JESUS, and Spouſe to MARY, who haſt the heart of à Father, and affection of à Spouſe, for thy true Clients; Unite your powerful interceſſion to Bleſſed Mary's, that our Adorable Redeemer ſweet JESUS, may caſt à propitious eye on them, obtain for me ſuch à filial confidence in thee; and ſuch à tender affection for thee, as JESUS and MARY had; that I may obtain his mercies, and your powerful aſſiſtance in all the exigences of this life, and the happy enjoyment of their, and thy company in the life to come. Amen.

And this to your good Angel.

O Moſt Holy Angel, my Guardian, my Maſter, my Guide, my Protector, and my moſt faithful Friend, to whoſe care I have been committed from the moment of my birth; teach me, govern me, and conduct me through the ſtrait, and ſecure way that leads to heaven, that by your aſſiſtance I may with you enjoy eternal life. Amen.

For the Evening Prayers, firſt ſay our Ladies Litanies.

The LITANY *of our Lady of* LORETTO.

LORD, have mercy on us.
Chriſt, have mercy on us.
Lord, have mercy on us.
Chriſt, hear us.
Chriſt, graciouſly hear us.
God the Father of Heaven, have mercy on us.
God the Son, Redeemer of the world, have mercy on us.
God the Holy Ghoſt, have mercy, &c.
O Holy Trinity, one God, have mercy on us.
Holy Mary, pray for us.
Holy Mother of God,
Holy Virgin of Virgins,
Mother of Chriſt,
Mother of Divine grace,
Mother moſt pure,

} Pray for us.

Mother most chaste,
Mother undefiled,
Mother untouched,
Mother most amiable,
Mother most admirable,
Mother of our Creator,
Mother of our Redeemer,
Prudent Virgin,
Venerable Virgin,
Renowned Virgin,
Powerful Virgin,
Merciful Virgin,
Faithful Virgin,
Mirrour of justice,
Seat of wisdom,
Cause of our joy,
Spiritual vessel,
Vessel of honour,
Vessel of singular devotion,
Mystical Rose,
Tower of David,
Tower of Ivory,
House of Gold,
Ark of the Covenant,
Gate of Heaven,
Morning Star,
Health to the weak,
Refuge of sinners,
Comfort of the afflicted,
Help of Christians,
Queen of Angels,

Pray for us.

Queen of Patriarchs,
Queen of Prophets,
Queen of Apoftles,
Queen of Martyrs,
Queen of Confeffors,
Queen of Virgins,
Queen of all Saints,

Pray for us.

O Lamb of God, that takeft away the fins of the world, fpare us, O Lord.

O Lamb of God, that takeft away the fins of the world, hear us, O Lord.

O Lamb of God, that takeft away the fins of the world, have mercy on us.

ANTHEM.

WE fly to thy patronage, O facred Mother of God, defpife not our prayers in our neceffities, but deliver us from all danger, O everglorious and bleffed Virgin.

℣. Pray for us, O holy Mother of God.

℞. That we may be made worthy of the promiffes of Chrift.

Let us Pray.

POur forth, we befeech thee, O Lord, thy grace into our hearts, that we, to whom the Incarnation of Chrift thy Son was made known by the meffage of an Angel, may, by his paffion and crofs, be brought to the glory of his Refurrection : Through the fame Chrift our Lord. Amen.

℣. May the Divine affiftance remain always with us. ℞. Amen.

℣. And may the fouls of the faithful, through the mercy of God, reft in peace. ℞. Amen.

℣. Pray for us Bleffed Saint JOSEPH;

℞. That we may be made worthy of the promiffes of CHRIST.

Let us Pray.

LEt us be affifted we befeech thee, O Lord, by the merits of the Spoufe of thy moft holy Mother, that what our own power doesnot obtain, may be granted us by his interceffion who liveft and reigneft world without end. Amen.

℣. Pray for us Bleffed Saint AUGUSTIN;

℞. That we may be made worthy of the promiffes of CHRIST.

Let us Pray.

BE favourable to our Petitions, almighty God; and fince thon encourageft us to hope in thy goodnefs mercifully grant us, by the interceffion of Bleffed Saint AUGUSTIN thy Confeffor and Bishop, the effect of thy ufual mercy. Through JESUS CHRIST our Lord. Amen.

H Y M N.

B Efore the cloſing of the day,
Creator we the humbly pray,
That for thy wonted mercy's ſake,
Thou us into protection take.

May nothing in our minds excite,
Vain dreams and phantoms of the night,
Keep off our enemies that ſo,
Our bodies no uncleanneſs know.

To JESUS from à Virgin ſprung,
Be glory given and praiſe ſung,
The like tho God the Father be,
And Holy Ghoſt eternally.

℣. Save us O Lord waking, and keep us
ſleeping.
℟. That we may watch with Chriſt, and reſt
in peace.
℣. Preſérve us as the apple of thine eye.
℟. And protect us under the shadow of thy
wings.
℣. Vouchſafe O Lord to keep us this night.
℟. Without ſin.
℣. Have mercy on us O Lord.
℟. Have mercy on us.
℣. Thy mercy be upon us O Lord.
℟. As we have put our truſt in thee.
℣. O Lord hear our Prayer.
℟. And let our ſupplication come unto thee,

Let us Pray.

VIfit we befeech thee O Lord, this habitation, and repel far from it all fnares of the
enemy, let thy Holy Angels dwell therein,
to preferve us in peace; and thy bleffing be
upon us for ever : through Chrift our Lord.
Amen.

O Angels of God, to whofe Holy care we
are committed by the fupream clemency, illuminate, defend, preferve, rule, and govern
us this night, and for ever more. Amen.

THE EXAMEN FOR NIGHT.

*WE muft remember that God who is every
where, is here prefent, and that he is the
abfolute Mafter of our lives ; let us then give
him à faithful account of his day ; and for
the firft point, adoring the Sacred wound in
our faviours right hand let us begin by thanksgiving for the benefits we have received from
that liberal hand.*

O Moft fweet JESUS! confidering your Sacred right hand, which you amoroufly gave
to your tormentors, to be moft cruelly pierc'd
with à nail for my Salvation : I moft humbly
thank your infinite Goodnefs, for all the benefits you have beftow'd upon me, both in
general and particular, efpecially this day,
and beg you to pardon me my paft ingratitu-

des, and negligences, in acknowledging my
obligations to you.

*For the second point, adoring the Sacred
wound in our Saviours left hand let us
beg light to discern our faults.*

BEholding dear Lord, your left hand
ſtretch'd out, and pierc'd to ſhew your liberality towards me ; I humbly beg light and
grace to know my faults and ſins; eſpecially
thoſe I have this day committed, that I may
be moſt heartily ſorry for them; as being offences againſt thy Divine, and amiable Goodneſs.

*For the third point, let us examen the faults
we have committed, either againſt God,
thoſe we depend on, our neighbour our ſelves. But firſt adoring the Sacred wound in
our Lords heart, let us ſay.*

WHen I contemplate my God! the prodigious opening of your Sacred heart, in which,
as in à furnace of love you have form'd the
deſigns of my ſalvation; even as in mine,
more cold than ice, the tranſgreſſions of your
divine counſels, and commandments have
been projected ; I think it moſt reaſonable,
O Divine Saviour, that I make my ſoul render an account of all the thoughts, words,
works, and omiſſons, whereby I have this
day any ways offended you,

EXAMEN OF CONSCIENCE.

I. Sins a gainſt God.

REmark 1. If at your awaking, you have given your firſt thoughts to God. 2. If you have not play'd, and talk'd inſtead of reciting the Prayers. 3. If you have heard Maſs with devotion. 4. If God has been the end to which you have referr'd all your actions. 5. If you have ſpent the day without thinking of God. 6. If you have perform'd what regards the ſervice of God with diſguſt, and repugnance.

II. Againſt thoſe you depend on.

1. IF you have been diſobedient to thoſe you depend on, in things they exact for your own Good. 2. If you have murmur'd at their commands. 3. If you have been angry at them, and have taken their corrections ill. 4. If you have not pay'd them à due reſpect. 5. If you have afflicted them by your indocility, and ill behaviour.

III. Againſt your neighbour.

1. IF you have hated, or yielded to an averſion for any. 2. If you have quarrel'd diſputed, made diſſentions, and told tales out of croſſneſs. 3. If you have anger'd others, deſpis'd them, diſedify'd them, excited them to do ill, or by your railleries hinder'd them

from doing Good. 4. If you have reproach'd any fpightfully , giving them nick, names , Judg'd rashly , of them , or detraĉted them. 5. If you have been Angry , Impatient , Crofs , Jealous , Sufpicious; and if out of Pride you have refus'd to yield to others. 6. If you have cenfur'd others aĉtions , or impertinently meddl'd with them.

IV. Againft your Self.

1. IF you have been Proud , and mov'd there-by , have exalted your felf above your Companions. 2. If you have held immodeft dif-courfes , or fung fuch fort of fongs. 3. If you have loft your time. 4. If you have fpent the day in railleries , foolish Jefts , or undecent words. 5. If in playing you have been to ru-de , or to eager , without moderation , taking pleafure to teafe others , to laugh exĉeffively , and to tell lies." 6. If you have in all things follow'd your paffions , and fenfualities.

For the fourth point , let us raife in our felves à true forrow for our fins , both in general , and in particular thofe of this day ; adoring the Sacred wound in our Lords right foot , and faying.

COnfidering dear Lord , with the eyes of my foul your Sacred right foot pierc'd with à nail; that foot , at which St. Mary Magda-

lene was converted; I muſt, O mercifull Judge
and Creator, let my heart break with grief
and contrition ; for I own I have moſt grie-
vouſly offended you, and therefore I deteſt
my ſins more than death and hell, principally
becauſe the are committed againſt your inſinit
and paternal Goodneſs : I purpoſe firmly with
your grace never to offend you more , to
amend my life, to confeſs my ſins, and to do
the penance which ſhall be enjoyn'd me.

*For the fifth point, let us more particularly
beg grace to amend , adoring the Sacred
wound of our Saviours left foot, ſaying.*

O My God , when I conſider by the light
of à lively faith, that when your left foot was
pierc'd, and nail'd, you were then nail'd to
the croſs to ſatisfie fully the rigorous juſtice
of your heavenly Father for my ſins, I moſt
humbly beſeech you from the bottom of my
heart, to grant me the grace to ſpend the remainder of my life without ever offending
you, and in performing ſuch an exact penance
for all my ſins, that I may deſerve to partake
of the fruit, and merits of your moſt Precious
Blood and Sacred Wounds ; and animated
with your ſpirit, ſuffer and die Crucify'd to
my pleaſures, that I may be entirely Sacrific'd
to your divine will , and poſſeſs you in your
glory for all eternity. Amen.

Then

Then for the Souls Departed.

FRom the depths I have cried to thee, O
Lord; Lord, hear my voice.

Let thy ears be attentive, to the voice of my
petition.

If thou wilt obferve iniquities, O Lord; Lord,
who shall fustain it.

Becaufe with thee there is Propitiation : & becaufe of thy law I have expected thee, O
Lord.

My foul has expected in his word, my foul
hath hoped in our Lord.

Becaufe with our Lord there is mercy : & with
him plentiful redemption.

And he shall redeem Ifrael from all his iniquities.

℣. Eternal reft give to them, O Lord :

℞. And let perpetual light shine upon them.

Lord have mercy on us.

CHRIST have mercy on us.

Lord have mercy on us.

Our Father &c.

℣. And lead us not into temptation.

℞. But deliver us from evil. Amen.

℣. From the gates of hell.

℞. Deliver their fouls O Lord.

℣. May they reft in Peace.

℞. Amen.

℣. O Lord hear my Prayer.

℞. And let my fupplication come unto thee.

C

Let us Pray.

O God the Creator & Redeemer of all the faithful, grant to the souls of thy servants departed, the remission of all their sins; that through pious supplications they may obtain that pardon which they have always defired who liveft & reigneft with God the Father in the unity of the Holy Ghoft one God, world without end. Amen.

℣. Eternal reft give to them O Lord.
℟. And let perpetual light shine upon them.
℣. May they reft in Peace. ℟. Amen.

A Hymn to our Bleſſed Lady.

O Star of Heaven whofe Virgin Breaft,
Thy fon our Lord did feed.
Who oft repelled, the deadly peft,
Caufed by firft man's mifdeed.
O thou aufpicious ftar reftrain,
The ftars contagious ills;
Whofe fell afpect, with ulcers pain :
Now threat, mankind to kill.
Moft pious fea ftar hear our cry,
From plague, thy fervants free;
For thee thy fon, will nought deny,
So much he honours thee.
Save us fweet JESUS, now & aye;
For whom, thy Virgin Mother deigns to
pray.

℣. Pray for us, O Holy Mother of God.

℞. That we may be made worthy of the promiſſes of CHRIST.

Let us Pray.

O God of piety, God of pardon, who haſt compaſſion on the affliction of thy people, & ſay'ſt unto the Angel ſtriking them; hold thy hand ; for the love of that glorious ſtar, whoſe precious breaſt againſt, the venom of our ſins, thou ſweetly ſuckeſt, grant the aſſiſtance of thy grace, that we may be preſerved from all plague & unprovided death, by thee O ſweet JESUS CHRIST, King of glory, who with the Father, & Holy Ghoſt, liveſt & reigneſt, world without end. Amen.

A PRAYER TO S. ROCH.

℣. Pray for us, Bleſſed Saint ROCH.

℞. That we may be made worthy of the promiſſes of CHRIST.

Let us Pray.

O Mnipotent, eternal God, who by the prayers & merits of thy Bleſſed Confeſſor St. ROCH, did ſtay a general peſtilence, grant unto us thy humble ſuppliants, who in like mortality, have recourſe unto thy divine Majeſty, by this thy by his merite & interceſſion

we may likewife be delivered from all plague
& peftilence. Through CHRIST our Lord and
Saviour. Amen.

When the Meditation has been read, fay.

COme Holy Ghoft, replenish the hearts of
the faithful, and kindle in them the fire of
thy love.

Whilft you undrefs your felf, which should
be with filence and modefty.

ENdeavour to diveft your felf of all the
ill habits, that fins and imperfections may
have left in you, by reflecting on the injury
they do to God, your Neighbour, and your
felf; and with a short prayer exprefs your
forrow and deteftation, begging grace to leave
them quite off.

AS FOR EXAMPLE.

IF you have been negligent and undevout
at your Prayers; think how difpleafeng that
is to God, who even curfes thofe that
do his work negligently; how difedifying to
your Neighbour, and how unprofitable and
difadvantagious to your felf; fince you not
only obtain nothing by fuch Prayers, but

alfo draw curfes upon your own head. Then
fay.

O My Dear Saviour! I am forry to think
how negligent and undevout I was at fuch,
and fuch à time; I deteft my ingratitude,
and beg grace that I may never more fall
into the like again.

If you have been disobedient to your

Miſtreſs.

THink how injurious that has been to God,
whofe place she bears in your regard. What
ill example you may have thereby given to
your companions, and how difadvantagious it
muft have been to your felf; fince certainly
she never requires any thing of you, but
what is for your own Good. Then fay, O
my dear Saviour &c. as before: only chan-
ging the name of the fault.

If you have quarrell'd with your

Companions.

THink how difpleafing that is to God,
whofe images they are, and who commands
you to love them. How difagreable, and
difedifying to your Neighbour, and how
difadvantagious to your felf, according to
that daily petition which you fay, *forgive us*

*our trefpaffus as we forgive them that tref-
pafs againft us &c.* Then fay the short Prayer
as before, or the like; ever naming the fault
you have been guilty of.

If you have loft your time.

THink how difpleafing that is to God,
who as given it you to labour in, for your
eternal falvation, how unprofitable both to
your Neighbour and your felf, and by confequence how difpleafing to your Parents,
who plac'd you here, to acquire virtue and
other decent improvements, which you will
never attain to by Idlenefs. Then fay the
short Prayer, as before.

In the like manner you may endeavour to
diveft your felf of any other ill habit, always
ftriving to excite in your felf affections, and
defires of the contrary virtue, embracing the
practife in all you can that night.

*Before you go to bed take Holy - water
and on your knees adore almighty
God, Saying.*

O My God, my Lord, and my Father! I
adore you with all the creatures which are
in heaven, and upon earth; acknowledging
you for my God and Souverain Lord, and

as I began this day by offering my self entirely to you, I defire alfo to finish it, in
confecrating to your Divine Majefty my body, foul, life, and all that I am : keep me
this night under your protection, and grant
that when my eyes are clos'd by fleep, my
heart may be ever open to your love, and
that after the shades and darknefs of this
life, I may attain to the happy day of eternity. Amen.

*Then recommand your felf to our Lady by
Some short Prayer, as.*

Mary, that Mother art of grace;
Of mercy Mother alfo art,
Save and defend us from our foe,
Receive us when we hence depart.

And ask her bleffing faying.

May the Virgin Mary obtain us the bleffing
of her divine Son.

*When you are in bed, write the name of
JESUS, on your forehead with your
thumb, and fay.*

O Moft fweet Jesus! in your name, and
for the love of you I go to fleep and repofe,
and humbly befeech your infinite Goodnefs,

to guard me this night from all evil, to protect me with your Holy benedictions, and
to conduct me to eternal life. Amen.

My God, grant that when my body repofes
in the fepulcher, y foul may repofe with
you in heaven. Amen.

Into thy hands O Lord! I commend my
fpirit.

*On communicating Eves from the half hour
after fix till feven, you fpend in vocal Prayers;
and hearing, or reading in the following of
Chrift; as the 21. chap. of the 1. book. the
4. 7. 8. of the 2. book. 4. 5. 10. 16. 31. 34. 59.
of the 3. book, and any in the 4. book.*

*For vocal Prayers, you may ufe the follo-
wing Prayers, or meditation.*

W Ho are you my Soverain Lord, and who
am I that I dare to approach you? What is
man of himfelf but à veffel of corruption, à
child of the devil, an heir to hell, an inftru-
ment of fin, an enemy of God, à ufelefs
creature as to Good, and unhappily powerful
in order to evil? What is man but an animal, blind in his defigns, vain in his actions,
Foul in his defires, unconftant in his defigns,
vile and bafe in all things, and only great
in the falfe efteem he has of himfelf? Shall

ſo miſerable à creature then dare to preſent her ſelf before à God of ſo infinite à Majeſty, for to unite her ſelf to him ?

O Lord ! the ſtars of heaven are not pure in your ſight, the pillars of heaven tremble in your preſence, the higheſt Seraphins cover themſelves with their wings before your greatneſs, and eſteem themſelves as nothing; how then shall à creature ſo miſerable as I am, undertake to touch you, and to receive you into her ſelf.

S. John Baptiſt ſanctify'd in the womb of his Mother, dares not touch your head, and proteſts that he is not worthy to untie your shoo's : the Prince of the Apoſtles cry's out, *Lord retire from me, becauſe I am à ſinner,* and shall I be ſo bold as to approach you, being full of ſin.

If in the time of the ancient law, it was needful to be pure and ſanctify'd to eat of the loaves expos'd on the table of your temple, tho' they were but à shadow of this miſtery, how can I but apprehend to eat the bread of Angels, being ſo bare of ſanctity as I am ?

You commanded my God, the Paſchal lamb to be eaten with unleaven'd bread, and bitter lettice, and that thoſe who eat it should have shoe's on their feet, and their reins girded ; and shall I dare to eat the true

Paſchal Lamb of which the other was but à figure, without having any thing of that preparation ? Am I bread without any leaven of malice ? Have I in me à true contrition, mark'd by the bitter lettice ? Where is the chaſtity of the reins, and cleannefs of the feet, which are good defires? I fear, and I have reaſon to fear to approach this Holy Table, feeing my ſelf ſo far from all thefe difpoſitions. An unhappy man was turn'd from it, becauſe he had not on the wedding garment, that is, Charity, he was commanded to be caſt into exteriour darkneſs bound hand and foot; and I can expeᏧ but the fame chaſtiſement, if I prefent my ſelf in the ſame condition, Divine eyes of my maſter, to which all the corners of our ſouls are difcover'd, what will become of me if I come thus naked to your feaſt?

If it was ſo great à crime for à Prieſt to have inconfiderately touch'd the ark of the teſtament which was ready to fall, that he was punifh'd on the fpot by à ſudden death, may I not well fear the fame pain, if I unworthily receive him that was figur'd by the ſame Ark. The Bethfamites did but to curiouſly look on that Ark when it pafs'd thro' their land; and the ſcripture tels us, that to expiate that temerity, God ſtroke with death fifty thouſand men of that people. O God! at once both merciful and terrible, how much is your Sacrament above that Ark; and what difference is there between receiving you, and looking on you? What muft I do to lodge in me à God, that is greatnefs and Juftice it felf?

But if I have fo much reafon to fear confidering only your Majefty, what ought I not to apprehend in regard of my fins? Infinite beauty! There was à time, (and mercifully grant it lafts not ftill,) when you were what my heart leaft thought of, and when I had more efteem for the duft of creatures; than for the treafures of your grace, and the hopes of your glory; my defires regulated my life, I blindly obey'd my concupifcences, and I made as little account of you, as if I had never known you. I have been that fool that faid in her heart: there is no God, becaufe I have liv'd long, as if I beliv'd there was none: I have never done any thing for your love, nor ever apprehended your juftice: I have never avoided evil for fear of your laws, nor ever return'd you due thanks for your benefits; and knowing you are every where, I have not refrain'd from finning in your prefence: I have granted to my eyes all they have defir'd, and have never given the leaft obftacle to my heart, to turn it from any pleafure. My life has been à continual oppofition and war againft you, and à renewing of all the

martyrdoms you have suffer'd for me. Shall I
then dare, my Saviour and my Judge, to receive you in this condition? I am confounded
at it, I am asham'd being what I am, to go
to the arms of the heavenly spouse, who vouch-
safes to embrace and receive me anew.

The second part.

O My God! I know my extream indignity,
and also know your great mercy; 't is what
gives me the boldness to approach you. As I
am, you are the more glorify'd by not rejecting so poor and impure à creature, you
do not turn sinners away; on the contrary,
you call and draw them to you : 't is you that
said, *come to me all you that are burthen'd
and afflicted, and I will solace you.* You
also said, *the Physician is not necessary to
the healthy, but to the sick : I am not come
to seek the Just, but sinners.* And it was pu-
blickly said of you, that you frequented sinners, and eat with them. You are still the
same you then were, and I believe you still
call from heaven, such as you then mercifully
call'd upon earth.

Mov'd then at the mercy, with which I
know you call us, I come to you loaden with
sins, that you may be pleas'd to ease me of
them : I come with all my miseries, and all

my temptations, to be folac'd by you : I come as à fick perfon to be cur'd by the Phyfician; and as à finner to the fountain of Juftice, there to be juftify'd. I hear that you receive finners, that you eat with them, and that your greateft delight is to converfe with them; if that be à nourriture pleafing to you, I being as I am, à great finner, you have in me fufficient to content your hunger.

I doubt 'not Lord, but that the tears of that publick finner Magdalene, were more pleafing to you, than the proud feaft of the Pharifee; fince you defpis'd not her gief, nor rejected her as à perfon defil'd with fin ; but on the contrary you accepted of her penance ; you pardon'd her offences, you defended her againft her accufers, and for à few tears, you remitted her many crimes.

Lord, fee here an occafion of acquiring you ftill more glory ; 'tis à finner who brings to your feet many more iniquities, and much fewer tears : you will not in this occafion shew the firft, nor the laft of your mercies ; you have already done the like many times, and will ftill often do it again : let this mercy I hope for, be of the number ; pardon me unhappy creature, who have more unworthily offended you, and have not fo much regret for my offences; I have not tears enough to wash your feet, but you have shed fo much

blood, that it is fufficient to wash away all
the fins of the world.

Be not angry my God, for that being,
fuch as you fee me, I prefume to approach
you : I know that all the fick ran to touch
you becaufe there came à virtue from you
which cur'd all I am taken with à dangerous
difcafe; what then can I do, but addrefs my
felf to you as to the moft powerful of reme-
dies, for the recovery of my health ? Your
being glorious in heaven, do's not make you
lefs merciful upon earth. In you Lord, is
health, life, and the remedy of all our miferies.

To whom then should we have recourfe in
our wants, if not to you Lord God?

I truly know that this Divine Sacrament,
is not only the food of the ftrong, but alfo
medicine of the infirm : that it is not only the
fupport of the living, but alfo the refurrection
of the dead : that it not only replenishes the
juft with love and Joy, but that it alfo puri-
fies and cures finners : that each approaches
as he can, and there receives what is proper
for him, and what his Lord is willing to give
him : that the juft come to be fed at this table, and that the voice of confeffion and praife
is heard for them in this Sacred feaft. But as
for me who am à finner and fick, I will come
to this divine banquet, to receive the Chalice
of falvation.

There is no way in the Chriftian life · by
which I can walk out of this Sacred Myftery,
and I fee not the leaft pretext to defend me
from wishing the participation thereof. If I am
fick, it will cure me, if I am well, it will
keep me fo, if I live, it will fortifie me, if I
am dead-it will reftore me to life. I will not
lofe courage for being blind, becaufe our Lord
gives fight to the blind; I. will not fly from
him like Adam when he perceiv'd his naked-
nefs, becaufe he is able to cover mine; I will
not hide my felf from him for being all defil'd
with fin, becaufe he is the unexhauftable fource of mercy; and in that, O my God! I do
not think I injure you; but on the contrary,
the more miferable I am, the more I think I
furnish you with à remarkable occafion, to
make your mercy be admir'd by ufing it towards me. The films that were on the eyes
of the man born blind, ferv'd but to make
the glory of God appear more refplendently
in him: and the low condition I am reduc'd
to, will more clearly show the goodnefs of
him, who being fo high, difdains not the
moft contemptible things: befides my merits
obtains not fo great à priviledge; but it is
granted me in confideration of thofe, of my-
Saviour JESUS CHRIST, for whofe fake the
Eternal Father adopts, and treats me as one
of his chrildren.

Since you are then my Father, and my
Saviour, I dare have recourfe to you; and
beg this grace, that as David let à deform'd
man fit at his table , becaufe he was Son to
his dear Friend Jonathas, by that means honouring the Fathers merits in the perfon of
the Son; fo you would pleafe alfo O Eternal
Father! to fuffer à poor disfigur'd finner at
yours , not upon her own account , but for
the merits of JESUS CHRIST, whom you
love fo much, who is our fecond Adam, our
true Father , and who with you lives, and
reigns for ever and ever. Amen.

*In the morning when you are to communi-
cate you go time enough to the Quire, that
you may at leaſt fay the morning Prayers
before Maſs Thenhear Maſs in this manner.*

*At the beginning of the Maſs, make the fign
of the Croſs, and then your intention
for communion, faying.*

O My God and my Saviour! I with all my
heart defire to receive you for your honour,
glory, in memory of your moft bitter paffion;
and that I may have the happineſs of being
united to you, and confecrate my felf entirely
to your fervice.

At

(49)

*At the CONFITEOR make Acts of
Contrition for all your sins, in this,
or the like manner.*

ACT OF CONTRITION.

O My moſt merciful Lord! proſtrate at the
feet of your Divine Majeſty, with all poſſible
ſentiments of regret and ſorrow; I moſt humbly beg pardon for all the ſins I have ever
committed, eſpecially thoſe ſince my laſt con-
feſſion : I deteſt them all in general, and each
in particular, becauſe they offend your goodneſs, and have cruelly put you to death.

*From the CONFITEOR till the Goſpel,
Produce Acts of humility, grounded upon
the conſideration of the greatneſs, power,
and Majeſty of him you are to receive, and
of your own baſeneſs, unworthyneſs, and
want of preparation.*

ACT OF HUMILITY,

O Almighty and everlaſting God ! before
whom all creatures of heaven, and earth
tremble with reſpect. What equality is there
between your Majeſty and my baſeneſs; your
omnipotence and my weakneſs; your ſanctity
and perfection, and my vices and defects,
that you honour me ſo highly as to come and

D

lodge with me, the moſt vile, and miſerable
of all your creatures : but ſince it pleaſes your
infinit greatneſs thus to abaſe it ſelf, I humbly accept of ſo great à mercy, tho' I am
very unworthy of it.

*If this, and the like is not ſufficient to
employ you till the Goſpel, you may make
uſe of that which is*, page 49.

At the Goſpel make Acts of Faith.

ACT OF FAITH.

MY God ! I believe all that is contain'd
in the Creed, and Holy Scriptures : and in
particular I confeſs with à firm faith, that
you are truly, and really preſent in the moſt
Bleſſed Sacrament of the Altar, vailing under
the ſpecies of bread and wine, your Body.
Blood, Soul, and all the grandeurs of your
Divinity, and tho' I do not clearly comprehend all theſe Divine Myſteries, ye ⸗ moſt
firmly believe them, becauſe that you who
are the firſt truth have reveal'd them to your
Church.

*From the Goſpel till SANCTUS, meditate
on theſe following points.*

1. Who you are to receive.
2. Who you are, that are to receive Him.
3. How he comes to you.

4. How you go to him.
5. Why he comes to you.
6. Why you go to him.

Or elfe you may meditate on fome point of the paffion; confidering the perfon that induces, his greatnefs and infinite excellence, the cruel torments he indures, the extream contempts he fuffers from all forts of perfons; and for whom he indures them for ungrateful creatures, unworthy of all good : from this confideration, excite your felf to à great confidence in the goodnefs of him, who has fuffer'd fo much for our falvation.

ACT OF HOPE.

O My moft liberal Lord! what may I not expect from the love which has mov'd you to fuffer, and indure fo much for me? O well may I now hope, that having given me your Blood and Life, you will not refufe me the graces which are the fruit of your death; efpecialy thofe that are neceffary for me to receive you in this divine Sacrament; which I confidently approach, being fure that you will help me in my neceffities, cure my infirmities, accomplifh my good defires, folace my pains, and replenish me with graces by your divine prefence.

After the SANCTUS, offer the Sacrifice in this manner.

O Eternal Father! I offer you the Holy, and Immaculate hoſt of the precious Body, and Blood of your beloved Son, which will be now immolated on this Altar : I offer it you my God, with the Prieſt who celeberates, in memory of the ineffable Miſtery of his Incarnation, of his moſt Holy life, of his dolorous Paſſion, and moſt precious Death. Receive alſo, O infinite Majeſty! this Holy Sacrifice for an eternal praiſe, in homage, and acknowledgment of the Souverain Dominion you have over me, and all creatures : in thanksgiving for your beneſits; in expiation of the ſins, both of the living, and of the faithful departed; and to obtain the ſpiritual, and temporal bleſſings which are neceſſary for us : but ſpecially to obtain of your goodneſs, requiſite diſpoſitions to receive you worthily.

At the Elevation, with a lively faith of this divine Miſtery, humbly adore your Saviour, ſaying.

MY Souverain Lord, and God, I adore you with the moſt profound humility, I wretched creature am capable off : and I reverence you with all my heart, in union of the Souverain adorations, that are now rendred you in heaven, and on earth by all your Elect.

*Then offer the eternal Father the sufferances
of his Son.*

ACT OF OFFERING.

LOok Lord on the face of your Chrift; behold his Sacred Body upon the Altar, and his
precious Blood in the Chalice : and tho' his
mouth fpeaks not a word, there are as many
mouths as wounds, which fpeak for me : fee
Lord, it is the fame Body which fweated blood
and water in the garden ; which was bound,
buffeted, and mock'd, whip'd, crown'd with
thorns, and infine crucify'd for my falvation :
I offer you all his fufferings, and conjure you
to apply the merits of them to my foul, giving
me graces neceffary to receive you worthily.

At the Pater nofter, *fay it with the Prieft
weighing particulaly this demand :* give us
this day our daily bread, *inftantly befeeching
the eternal Father, to give us this living
bread defcended from heaven, to give life to
the world.*
*Then what time remains till the Poft-Commu-
nion, you may employ in vocal Prayers,
efpecially fuch as are proper for before Communion. And from the Poft-Communion till
you go to receive, make acts of love, and
of an ardent defire to communicate.*

O My moft amiable Saviour ! you have never teftify'd with fuch excefs, your divine

goodnefs, and your infinite charity as in this
Sacrament of love; grant then that I may love
you with all my heart, and with all my for-
ces, becaufe of the love and goodnefs you
therein teftifie to me. Why have I not all the
hearts and wills of men and Angels, to love
you more perfectly?

A c t o f D e s i r e.

O Come my only Good! come to me, for
I ardently defire to receive you; come quickly
then, and by your corporal entrance into my
body, pafs into my foul which has no life
without you.

D e s i r e o f D i s p o s i t i o n s.

O That I had the difpofitions, with which
your Bleffed Mother recev'd you into her Sacred womb at your Incarnation; and could
approach you with the reverence that the
Bleffed Virgin, and all the Saints have brought
to this Auguft Sacrament.

A P r a y e r t o o u r L a d y.

O Holy Mother of God! I addrefs my felf
to you, that you would pleafe to make me
partake of the great, and fublime difpofition
you us'd to have, when you receiv'd your
dear Son in this Holy Sacrament.

To your Angel Guardian.

O My moſt Holy Angel Guardian, have
Compaſſion on my inability to do this action
worthily, and aſſiſt me I beſeech you, with
your favorable ſuccours.

In Saying the Confiteor, *make an Act of
Contrition for your diſtractions and negligence
in preparing your ſelf; beſeeching our Lord
that thro' his infinit mercy, he would efface
what ſpots may yet remain on your ſoul.*

*In going to Communion, endeavour to en-
liven your faith of the real preſence in the
Bleſſed Sacrament. Then make an act of re-
ciprocal love in the moſt fervorous manner
you can poſſibly.*

An Act of Reciprocal Love.

O Fire of charity! why can I not approach
you with the ſame love, which moves you
to come to me? I love you my God, but I
love you not enough ; grant me then the
grace to love you more. Lord open to me
the arms of your goodneſs, and receive with
mercy her, who goes to receive you with
confidence and love.

*After Communion, you beſtow the time of
a Maſs, or half an hour, in thanksgiving
for great a benefit, and enjoying the ſweet*

*preſence of our Lord; making great account
of each moment of time he remains with you,
ſince in each he may beſtow great favours,
if entertain'd as he should be. To which effect you may produce divers affections and
acts of virtue, particularly of Admiration,
Humility, Adoration, Offering, Thanksgiving and Petition, both for your ſelf, and
you, neighbours.*

HUMBLE ADMIRATION.

IS it poſſible that God dwells in my heart?
That he whom the heavens cannot contain,
is shut up in my breaſt? O God of Soverain
Majeſty! Do you thus give your ſelf to be
eaten by à worm? You that are Monarch of
all the world, do you thus abaſe your Grandeur to this Abyſs of miſery? And who am
I that you should ſo much as vouchſafe to remember me? O ineffable communication! O
exceſs of Goodneſs!

ADORATION.

MY Amiable Saviour, acknowledging your
divine excellence, I caſt my ſelf at the feet
of your Majeſty, and adore you as the only
Son of God, my firſt beginning, my Soverain good, and my laſt end. O how happy
do I eſteem my ſelf to depend thus totally on

you! I adore you again with all my heart, and with all the Affections of my foul : why can't I adore you in the manner your Holy Mother, the Angels, and all the Celeſtial Citizens, adore you in heaven?

Offering.

MY God! I am already yours by an infinity of titles, and offering my felf to you, I do but reſtore you your own; but the ineſtimable preſent you have now made me, in giving me your felf, makes me wiſh to be ſtill more perfectly yours : therefore I confecrate to you my foul, and all its powers, my body, and all its fenfes, my heart with all its affections : I alſo offer you my life, my health, my ſtrength, my pretenfions, all that I am in the order of nature or grace; all that I can, all that I shall do, think, and ſay for ever.

Thanksgiving.

O My moſt liberal and mercyful Lord, I return you millions of thanks, for that without regard to my unworthyneſs, you have been pleas'd to give me your Sacred Body, your Precious Blood, your moſt Holy Soul, your Adorable Divinity, and this ineffable preſent with an infinite Love. May all the Blef-

ſed Spirits praiſe you for it with me, and may
all creatures bleſs, and thank you for ſo incomparable à benefit.

Benedicite omnia opera Domini Domino &c.

*Do'nt forget to unite your acts of thanks-
giving to thoſe that our Saviour render'd to
his Father when upon earth, particularly
after the laſt ſupper, and the inſtitution of
this Divine Sacrament. Do the ſame in all
the other acts.*

PETITION.

O My moſt mild and liberal Saviour ! you
never enter'd any place upon earth without
leaving marks of your liberality behind you ;
and will you not uſe the ſame mercy being
now in me ? I conjure you to it O infinite
Goodneſs ! and beſeech you with all my heart,
to operate in my ſoul the effects of your coming : do not mind my unworthyneſs, nor
the ſmall preparation with which I have receiv'd you, but pardon me O my amiable Saviour, all theſe negligences, and the other ſins
and defects I have committed againſt you.

Grant me alſo my God, the grace to love
you perfectly, and to die rather à thouſand
times, than to offend you by one only mortal
ſin. Grant I may in all things accomplish your

moſt Holy will, and renounce my own when
contrary to it; give me moreover I beſeech
you, ſtrength to reſiſt temptations, and courage to overcome my paſſions, and ill habits,
eſpecially N. and N. *here ſpecifie the chief,
together with your other wants and neceſſities,
amorouſly and confidently diſcovering them to
our Lord, that he may remedy them.*

*This being done you may employ ſome time
in vocal Prayers, in devout lectures on the
ſubject of Communion, and in gaining the indulgences if you have medals. And do not
forget to pray for the Holy Church, for the
King, and union of Chriſtian Princes, for
your Parents, Friends, and Benefactors, as
well living as dead, and alſo for the other
ſouls in Purgatory, eſpecially thoſe that are
moſt forſaken; and if you have Indulgences
you may apply them to them.*

A PRAYER AFTER COMMUNION.

O My Saviour JESUS CHRIST! O True Son
of God! O ineffable Goodneſs! O Bread of
Angels! O Divine Manna! O my Soverain
Good! O Venerable Sacrament! O moſt Holy
Soul of JESUS! O Sacred Body of my Saviour!
O Precious Blood! O Price of my redemption!
O infinite Treaſure! O Good JESUS! I render
you à thouſand millions of thanks, for that

you have nourish'd and fed me with your Sacred Body and Blood.

Alas! what can I more defire, fince I poffefs you in my foul? Ah my God! let me never more be feparated from you : You have given your felf wholly to me, I alfo give my felf entirely to you. O Fire of charity! O Divine Food! O Salutary Hoft! Difperfe the darknefs of mind, illuminate the eyes of my underftanding to know you, enflame my heart to love you, and make me in all things accomplish your Holy will. Amen.

Endeavour to behave your felf the reft of the day with à great deal of circumfpection and modefty, remembering the infinite bleffing you have receiv'd, and by your actions shewing the efteem you have of it.

If you have time you may after Communion, meditate on thefe points.

1. Who you have receiv'd.
2. Who you are that have receiv'd him.
3. What he can do for you.
4. What you ought to do for him.
5. What he defires to do for you.
6. What you will do for him.
7. What you shall ask of him.
8. What you shall offer him.

In time of the hours fay your hours, our

Ladies office (or the morning Prayers according to the day of the week , you have in your manual) and your beads if you have time ; except it be on à feaſt of our Lady , or the firſt ſunday of the month , for then you ſay the roſary all together in the ſchool.

At Veſpers you ſay our Ladies office &c. , as on other days.

At Salüe renewing the remembrance of your morning happyneſs , Yoy may produce theſe followings acts.

Act of Faith.

I Firmly believe my God , that you are here preſent; and would rather doubt of my being , and life , than of this great truth.

And tho' this Miſtery should be à thouſand times more incomprehenſible then it is , having your word , I would not doubt of it in the leaſt. O how agreable is this darkneſs to me , which gives me an occaſion to humiliate my underſtanding under your verity!

I caſt my ſelf at your feet , O my moſt amiable Saviour! with the tears and love of Magdalene , and beg as true à ſorrow for my fins as this Holy Penitent , and faithful lover had.

Then with admiration of his Goodneſs , ſay.

BUt is it you my God , who are on high in the ſplendours of you glory? Yes 'tis you,

O true, O beft of Friends, and the only
friend I have in the world; other friends embrace to shew their love, and you enter into
the bottom of my hear to teftifie yours.

What joy! what h ynefs to poffefs you!

Is there any thing t : can feparate me from
you? No I hope by our grace, that all the
powers of hell will ver be able to do it.

Act of Thanksgiving.

WHat shall I give you, O my Saviour! in
acknowledgment of fo many favours? For the
Empire of heaven and earth is already yours :
O if you wanted any thing that I could buy
with the prife of all the blood in my veins,
how willingly would I give it! But you have
need of nothing, being infinitly infinite in all
fort of good : I give you my heart, my eyes,
my tongue, and all my fences and powers,
making you Mafter of all my goods, that you
may difpofe of them as you pleafe; I give you
my life, and having an infinity of moments
in it, I wish I could glorifie you as much in
each moment, as the Angles and Saints have
ever, or shall ever glorifie you in all eternity.
I give my felf to you for à flave, that you may
difpofe of me wherever, and how you pleafe :
infine my God accept me as à victime, fince
I defire to die, and be reduc'd to ashes for
your glory.

Act of the love of Complaifance.

I Rejoyce that this Divine Saviour of mine
is fo amiable ; yes my God I rejoyce at your
infinite perfections, that you are infinitly Holy,
infinitly happy, infinitly wife, and infinitly
powerful.

Act of the love of benevolence.

I Wish I could, tho' it coft me my life, fee
all men know, love, adore à God fo good and
fo amiable, and that no body ever offended him.

Act of the love of preference.

MY God! I make more account of the leaft
thought that raifes, and conducts me to you,
than of all the Empires of heaven and earth,
with all their richefs, and delights.

Act of the love of conformity.

I Had rather die my God, than feparate my
felf from your Holy will : O let me know what
you would have me do, and I'll pafs thro'
fire and water to perform it.

Act of Defire.

I Defire to love JESUS perfectly, to glorifie
him moft highly, and purely for his love ;
above all, and with all the poffible love of all

poffible creatures; without limits in all he or-
dains, in all he permits, for my whole life,
and for an eternity entire ; with an infatiable
defire to love him for ever more ardently, and
more perfectly, becaufe he deferves to be lov'd
with an infinite love.

Act of confidence to obtain great graces.

Since O my Saviour, you have given me all
the beft you have in giving me your felf, you
cannot refufe me fuch, and fuch things.

*Act of Confeffion, for that our Lord during
the 33. years of his life, never enter'd any
place without leaving marks of his prefence
by fome particular grace.*

Alas! entering fo many times into me, I
feel fmall effects of it; my indifpofitions, my
affections, my paffions and negligences, hinder the effects of your infinite Goodnefs.

Act of à moft humble Prayer.

I Befeech you my God, by all your infinite
Goodnefs, by the love which nail'd you to
the Crofs, and annihilates you in this Sacrament, leave in me fome mark of your divine
vifit; give me fuch, and fuch à grace, à great
fervour in your fervice ; mortifie in me fuch
and

and fuch paffions, which hinder my perfection; put your felf as à feal upon my poor
heart, that it may have your fentiments, and
delight no more in any thing, but what is
pleafing to you.

*Then you may lead our Saviour thro' all
your powers and fenfes : show him the diforders you find in them, the violences of your
paffions, the diforders of your fenfes, and of
your wild imagination, the darknefs of your
underftanding, the weaknefs, and inconftancy
of your will, the forgetfulnefs of your memory, the abufe of his benefits, your fpiritual
poverty. Befeech him to reform all, to make
you a new creature, and to fanctifie you entirely.*

*Then keep, or attentively read this
Meditation.*

IF all creatures in heaven and earth were
chang'd into tongues, and join'd with me to
give thanks for the benefit you have beftow'd
on me my God, they could not do it as you
deferve : O my Saviour! what praife shall I
give you, for having been pleas'd this happy
day, to vifit me, to comfort me, and to
honour me with your prefence? When the
Mother of your precurfor full of the Holy
Ghoft, faw the Virgin enter her houfe, who

E

bore you in her womb , she being aſtoniſh'd
with ſo great a wonder cry'd out : *whence is
this happineſs to me that the Mother of my
Lord comes to viſit me ?* What muſt I then
do who am but a worm, ſeeing that my mouth
has receiv'd , and that my breaſt has lodg'd
the ſame God that came to viſit Saint Eliſa-
beth? With how much more reaſon may I
cry out , how comes this extraordinary favour,
that not only the Mother of my God , but
that my God himſelf has been pleas'd to viſit
me , who have been ſo long à dwelling place
for ſatan , who have ſo often offended him ,
who have always oppos'd his deſigns, and by
rejecting him ſo many times , have render'd
my ſelf wholly unworthy to receive him ?
Whence then is this grace to me , that the
Lord of Lords ſhould come to me?

You have been pleas'd O my King ! to be
born amongſt beaſts, to be deliver'd into the
hands of ſinners, and to deſcend even to hell :
't is plain my God that you keep ſtill the ſame
love for ſinners, ſince you yet daily do what
you once did in their favour.

If you had vouchſaf'd to approach me in
ſome other manner it had been à very great
mercy; but Lord , you have not only been
pleas'd to viſit me , but you have daign'd to
enter into me, to ſtay in me, to transform me
into you, and to make me one and the ſame

thing with you; this is what surpasses human
wit : David wonder'd that you would so much
as remember man, and fix your heart upon
so poor à creature; but it is much more wonderful that God not only remembers man,
but that he makes himself man for him, remains with him, and for him, nourishes him
with his own substance, and makes himself
one, and the same thing with him. May the
Angels bless you then my God, for so high
à grace, and so incomparable à Goodness.
Let me love you then dear Lord, and desire
you above all things : be you my meat and
drink, O Amorous Sweetness! O Love inesti-
mably sweet! Let my soul feed on you, O
Meat more delicious than all the delights of
the earth! Nourishment of the poor, make
me grow in you; augment what your presence
puts in me, to the end I may be worthy
happily to enjoy you. Children of Adam,
blind men, what do you do? What do you
pretend to in the world ? If you seek love,
here is the noblest and sweetest that can be
wish'd for : if you desire pleasures, where can
you find greater and purer than these ? If you
would have wealth, here is the treasure of
heaven, the price of the world, and an ocean
of riches : Infine if you aspire to honours,
you will here find the Majesty of God, who
comes to honour you.

Second part of the Meditation.

SInce you have already done me the honour to receive me into your company, to give me place at your table, to let me partake of your careffes, and to bind me to you with fuch ftrong and ftrait bands of love, I from this moment, O my Saviour! renounce all other loves for the love of you : let there be no more world, nor no more vanity for me : away falfe goods, which I have lov'd too much; here is the only and Soverain good; 'twould be unreafonable after having tafted the bread of Angels, to return to the food of beafts ; 'twould be injuft after having receiv'd God into my houfe, to let any vain and unprofitable thing enter : if a King had efpous'd a perfon of mean condition, that perfon would foon quit her ftate of poverty, to appear like a Queen. 'Tis what my foul has now to imitate ; for after having been exalted to the dignity this Auguft Sacrament has eftablish'd her in, can fhe refolve to abafe her felf agaid in the infamous ftate her old habits had reduc'd her too?

·Since you have been pleas'd my Saviour, to honour me with a vifit, give me the grace in fome fort to correfpond with the favour : You have never done any extraordinary favours to any without granting them powerful

fuccours at the fame time, and if by your
adorable prefence I have receiv'd of you an
honour that furpaffes all others, let your Soverain power fanctifie me, that I may be able
to fatisfie my obligations. Where ever you
have enter'd, you have ftill proceeded in this
merciful manner : You enter'd the chafte womb
of your Bleffed Mother, and as you thereby
exalted her to an eminent glory, you alfo at
the fame time gave her moft high grace to
fuftain it. Being ftill shut up in that Holy
Sanctuary, you enter'd Saint Elifabeth's houfe, and by your prefence, you fanctifi'd her
Son, gaue him à heavenly joy, and replenish'd his Mother with your fpirit. You enter'd the world to converfe with men; and
as by your coming upon earth you rais'd them
to a marvellous degree of honour, fo by a
marvellous grace you repair'd their defects,
and fanctifi'd them when they were wicked :
Infine you defcended into hell, and of that
hell you made a Paradife, making thofe Bleffed by your prefence, whom you honour'd
with a vifit.

'Tis not only you Lord that have done
thefe wonders : the Ark of the teftament
which was but a shadow of this miftery, enter'd the houfe of Obededom, and prefently
you pour'd your benedictions on it, an all
that belong'd to that good Ifraelite. Since

then you are pleas'd by a greater mercy , to
enter so poor a dwelling as that of my foul ,
and to remain in it, begin to bless the house
of your servant , and give me wherewith to
correspond to that grace. Enrich and adorn
your habitation, make it worthy of you. You
would have me be like that happy sepulcher
where your Sacred Body was plac'd; give me
then I beseech you its qualities : it was of
stone, give me constancy ; there was a Sin-
don in it which represents humility , grant me
that virtue my God, since so necessary for
me; there was myrrh in it which is the sym-
bol of mortification ; grant that I may die
my God, to all my irregular desires , and to
my own will , and that I may live to you
alone. In establishing your abode in me , you
design'd to have me like the Ark of the testa-
ment ; grant me then this favour, that as it
contain'd nothing but the tables of the law ,
my heart may contain no other thoughts, nor
desires but those of conforming entirely to
your law. You let me know by the effects of
this great Sacrament , that you are my Father, since you treat me in it as your Child;
but as being your Child, give me your grace
that I may worthily correspond with this benefit, in loving you not only with à strong
and solid love , but also with à love full of tenderness. May all my powers melt and plunge

themselves, in your love , and may the only
remembrance of your most sweet and amiable
name, make all the joy of my heart ; let all
my hope and confidence be in you, and in
all labours and pains of this life, I shall have
recourse to you as a Good Child, who casts
himself into the arms of his Father, where he
finds his most secure refuge. But above all
you have been pleas'd to discover to me in
this Mistery , that you have for my soul all
the love a tender spouse can have for his belov'd spouse : give me a like heart for you;
let my affection answer yours; let my love be
like yours, faithful, chaste, and tender; and
let it be so strong and powerful, that never
any thing may separate me from you.

O most chaste spouse of our souls! open your
divine arms , and bind my soul to you with
such strong bands, that in life and death, I
may remain inseparably fasten'd to you : you
ordain'd this Divine Sacrament to form that
so strait an union; for you know that the creature is much better in you , than her self,
that she has from you all her strength and
power; that of her self she is nothing but misery and weakness; that without you she lo-
ses her self like to a drop of water , which
being left alone in the air dries up in à moment, but being cast into the sea and united
to its principle, is always conserv'd. Draw me

then from my felf my God, and receive me into you, becaufe in you I find life, and in me death. I become ftrong in you, and wafte away in my felf : being in you I acquire a ftable and fixt ftate, and of my felf I am but vanity and corruption. Leave me not then O Good JESUS! leave me not Lord! but tarry with me, becaufe the day is far fpent, and the night approaches : and fince I have been fo happy as to lodge you to day in my houfe, where I can treat with you alone of my fouls concerns, I will not lofe fo favorable an occafion, nor let you efcape me, till you have given me your benediction : change my old name and give me a new one, that is to fay, a new being, and a new fort of life.

Make me lame of one leg like Jacob, and let the other remain found and vigorous; that is, let the love of the world grow daily weaker in me, and yours remain entire, and ftrong as long as I live, to the end that having extinguish'd in me all other loves, and all earthly defires, I may love you only, O my Saviour! defire you only, think of you only, and dwell with you alone : let me not live but for you; may all my thoughts and cares regard you? May I have my fole recourfe to you in all my labours, and neither expect, nor receive any fuccour but from you? Who liveft and raigueft for ever and ever. Amen.

A Prayer to adore the most Blessed Sacra-
ment, and to repair the injuries our
Lord there receives.

O My JESUS, my God, and my Saviour!
true God, and true man most worthy victime
of the most High, Living bread, and source
of eternal life, I adore you with all my heart
in this Divine Sacrament, with design to repair
all the irreverences, profanations, and impie-
ties which have been committed against you
in this dreadful Mistery. I prostrate my self
before your Divine Majesty, there to adore
you in the name of all those who have never
paid you any duty, and who perhaps will be
so unhappy as never to render you any; as
Hereticks, Atheists, Blasphemers, Magicians,
Jews, Idolaters, and all Unbelievers. I wish
my God, I could give you as much glory,
as they would altogether pay you; if they
faithfully render'd you their respects, and ack-
nowledgments; and I wish I could collect in
my faith, in my love, and in the Sacrifice of
my heart, all the honour, love, and glory,
they might have been capable of rendering
you in the extent of all ages, were they converted : which inestimable grace I implore of
you for them.

I even most ardently desire to give you as
many benedictions and praises, as the damn'd

will difcharge injuries againft you in all the
length of their torments; and to fanctifie this
adoration, and make it more agreeable to you,
I unite it, O my Saviour! to all thofe of your
Univerfal Church in heaven and earth.

Regard the fentiments of my heart, rather
than the words of my mouth, for I mean all
that your Holy fpirit infpires your Bleffed Mother, and your Saints with , to honour you,
and all that you fay your felf to your Eternal
Father, in this glorious and Auguft Sacrament, where you are his perpetual Holocauft,
and in the divine bofom, where he engenders
you from all eternity, and where you praife
him infinitely.

*On Sundays and Holy-days when you don't
communicate., being come to the Quire make
your adoration, as page 1●. then fay the
morning Prayers, and after that beftow at
leaft a quarter of an hour in meditation, in
which you may ufe this method.*

Having read it over night to fee what virtue you may moft want, of thofe, that the
fubject of your Meditation directs to, chufe it
for the fubject of your Prayer : and give due
time in fully recollecting your felf in the prefence of God, by the confideration of his prefence, Majefty, power, greatnefs, your dependance on him, his goodnefs &c.

And always by way of fecond prelude, beg
of him the knowledge, efteem, love, and
gift of that virtue, which you have taken for
the fubject of your Prayer. Then if you feel
any particular motion from God, or affection
in your heart, freely take as much time as
you can, or all, in entertaining it. When
you do not, let the four points of your Meditation ever be.

1. All the motives that can raife efteem or
defire, of that virtue.

2. What one in your circumftances, that
were refolv'd to practife and obtain that virtue, would do.

3. Whether you do fo, and take a view of
all your faults againft it, with a fence of contrition.

4. What you will do hereafter, of all the
purpofes relating to that virtue. Laftly fpend
the reft of the time in earneft Prayer, or petitions, concerning it.

Three reflections to be made after Prayer.

1. With what refpect and reverence do you
adore God : by a lively act of faith, follow'd
by an entire oblation and Sacrifice of your
felf?

2. What atract do's your Prayer incline you
to, as humility, patience, penance, confidence, love, &c. ? What have been your affec-

tions? Or have you been in aridity, dulnefs, diftractions? And how have you comported your felf in them? With what humility, patience &c.

3. Do you conclude with due thanksgiving? What colloquies, and refolutions of ferving God more perfectly?

Chufe fome afpiration drawn from the fubject of your Meditation; which may the reft of the day., from time to time petition Gods mercy to obtain the virtue, or overcome the vice, as your prefent neceffity requires.

At the Elevation of the Hoft.

M Oft Adorable Body! I adore thee with all the powers of my foul. Lord, who haft given thy felf entire to us ; grant we may become entirely thine.

The fame Eternal word who brought all things at firft out of nothing, he that faid, *let there be light*, and .there was light : *let the earth bring forth its fruits*, and it was fo; the fame Eternal word now fays, this is my Body; and fpeaks it from the higheft heavens, at this very moment, by. the voice of his fervant.

At the Elevation of the Chalice.

M Oft Adorable Blood, that wafheft away all our fins! I adore thee : happy we if we can return our life and blood for thine.

Then confidering the thoughts that JESUS CHRIST may have of us, and thofe he has for us; that is to fay, the difpofition of his heart, his defires, his defigns, &c. penetrated with a true fenfe of gratitude, and tendernefs, you may produce the following act.

BE pleas'd, O Eternal Father! that I offer you the Sacred heart of JESUS CHRIST, your beloved Son, as he offers himfelf a Sacrifice to you; receive for me all the defires, fentiments, affections, motions, and acts of this Sacred heart: they are all mine, fince 'tis for me he immolates himfelf; they are mine, fince I intend to have no other from henceforward, but his: receive them in fatisfaction for all my fins, and in thanksgiving for all your benefits; receive them, to grant me by their merit all neceffary graces, efpecially the laft and final grace; receive them intine as fo many acts of love, adoration, and praife which I offer your Divine Majefty, fince it is by him only, that you are worthily lov'd, honour'd and glorifi'd: *quoniam per ipfum, & cum ipfo, & in ipfo, eft tibi Deo Patri omnipotenti, in unitate Spiritus Sancti, omnis honor & gloria.*

Then you may fay the hours of our Ladies office; or if you do'nt fay it, the morning

*Prayers in your Manual according to the day
of the week, or any other vocal Prayers, as
your beads &c. but remark that the times,
when you may fit down in a finging Mafs
are, in time of the Epiftle; after the Prieft
has faid the* Gloria in Excelfis, *and* Credo;
*whilft the Quire is finging them, and after
the Communion till the Poft-Communion. In
reading maffes, if you cannot kneel up all
the time as the dignity of the miftery requires, you may fit in time of the Epiftle; from
the Creed till the Preface; and after the Communion of the Prieft, till the Poft-Communion.*

1. THe beft method of hearing Mafs, is to
be prefent at it in the fpirit of the Church,
which is the fame with that of Chrift, in offering his facrifice upon Mount Calvary; of
which that of the Altar, is a memory, and
the very fame victime.

2. Our Bleffed Lords fpirit was that of an
entire Sacrifice; there being four fort of Sacrifices. 1. Of Holocauft, only to adore, wors-
hip, and praife the Soverain Greatnefs, and
Goodnefs, of God. 2. Of thankſgiving, for
the continual favours and graces we receive.
3. Impetratory, to crave and obtain fuch graces and gifts as we ftand in need of 4. Propitiatory, to obtain forgivenefs of fins : our

Bleffed Lord comprehended all thefe four forts
of Sacrifices in his.

3. Our dependance on God lafting every
moment; we should every moment adore and
glorifie him. He beftowing continually new
graces and favours upon us, we ought likwife
every moment to offer up à Sacrifice of Thanksgiving to him. Our wants being continual;
Each moment alfo would require an Impetratory Sacrifice. Infine our offences being every
moment with an uncertainty whether any paft
onés be remitted ; each moment of our life
would alfo require from us a propitiatory Sacrifice. Any one of thefe duties is impoffible
to us, much more all : in this therefore confifts the admirable bleffing of the Holy Mafs,
that Chrift our Lord by it, fulfills for us all
our obligations to his Eternal Father, in an
infinitly perfeðt manner; infinitly beyond all,
that all Saints and Angels could do during
all eternity, towards complying with only any
one of thefe duties : and therein lies our moft
precious treafure.

4. *Chrift then offering for us thofe four Sacrifices in each Mafs; our duty is to offer
them with him. Therefore at the fecond Mafs
on Sundays and Holydays ufe this method.*

From the beginning to the offertory, looking on it as a Propitiatory Sacrifice for our
fins, offer it as fuch ; and join with it all the

acts of confessing your sins to God , Contrition , Humiliation , and petition of forgiveness, which your devotion can suggest.

From the Offertory to *Sanctus* , looking on it as a Thanksgiving Sacrifice, offer it as such ; join to it all memory of receiv'd favours , with most fervent thanks, and return of Good purposes , as a grateful acknowledgment.

From *Sanctus* to the *Pater noster*, looking on it as a Holocaust to glorifie and praise Gods Soverain Greatness, and Goodness, offer it as such; especially at the elevation , join your praises and adorations of the divine attributes, together with the adorations of all the Angels and Saints in heaven.

From the *Pater noster* to *Agnus Dei* , offer it as Impetratory; begging with a lively faith, all you feel most want off, not forgetting your neighbours, nor the necessities of the holy Catholick Church.

Then spiritual Communion : and in the time of S. John's Gospel, give grateful thanks to our Lord , for so mercifully fulfilling all your duties and obligations.

In time of the hours, if you don't go to catechism you may read some good book.

At Vespers as before page 24.

At Salüe, first with à profound reverence
make this Act of Adoration.

O JESUS! my Lord and God! whom I
believe to be truly and realy prefent in the
moft Bleffed Sacrament of the Altar : receive
this act of à moft profound Adoration, to fupply for the defire I should have of continually
adoring you there ; and in thanksgiving for
the fentiments of love, that your Sacred heart
has for me : I offer you all the Acts of Adoration, Refignation, Patience, and Love, that
your Sacred heart made during your mortal
life, and that it ftill makes, and will eternally
make in heaven ; to the end to adore you,
love and praife you, as much as is poffible for
me by that Sacred heart, during the whole
courfe of my life.

O my Saviour! open that divine heart unto
me, and it shall from henceforward be the
place of refuge, and of my reft.

ACT OF LOVE.

I Have nothing, O my amiable Saviour, and
my God! I have nothing that can pleafe you;
I can do nothing, nay, I am nothing; but I
have à heart, and that fuffices me. I may be
depriv'd of health, honour, and life it felf,
but I cannot lofe my heart : I have à heart,
and with this heart I can love you, O my
Adorable JESUS! and with this heart I will

F

love you, O my God ! I will love you and
will always love you here, that I may for ever
love you hereafter.

ACT OF CONTRITION.

O My Saviour, and my God ! whose heart
wounded with love and grief, had such regret for all the sins of the world : why can
I not resent the same grief that mine has
caus'd you ? Supply I beseech you, by the
contrition you had for them, what is wanting
in mine : Imprint in my heart à horrour , and
fear of the lightest offences : change and reform this unhappy heart by the modle of yours,
infinitly pure, Soverainly Holy, and ever enflam'd with the love of your heavenly Father;
for I protest that for the future I will only love
what it loves , as I detest all that is displea-
sing to it. Amen.

*A Prayer that St. Gertrude recited daily
in honour of the Sacred heart
of JESUS.*

I Salute you O Sacred heart of JESUS, lively
and enlivening source of eternal life , infinit
treasure of the Divinity, burning furnace of
divine love ; you are my rest and sanctuary :
O my amiable Saviour ! enflame my heart
with the ardent love which burns your; pour
into my heart the graces which yours is the

source of; and grant that it may be so united
to yours, that your will may be mine, and
that mine may be eternally conformable to
yours; since I desire that for the future your
Holy will may be the rule of all my desires
and actions. Amen.

Act of Love.

GIve me leave to address my self to you!
O divine and adorable heart of JESUS my Saviour! Abyss of love and mercy; and permit
me to ask you, seis'd with astonishment at
the sight of your Goodness, and my ingratitudes; why O my God! have you invented
this new way of immolating your self for me
in the divine Eucharist? Do you dear Lord,
so little account your having once offer'd your
self to torments, and death? Must I, now you
are glorious and immortal, continually see you
expos'd to approbries in this your Sacrament
of love, where you are so often despis'd; in-
sulted, and trod under foot, even by those
who ought to love you most ardently? And
must I see my self in the number of these
miserable ungrateful creatures, and not die
with grief and confusion? Ah my God! Pierce
my heart with the dart of your love, and put
an end to my ingratitudes. Remember Lord
that your adorable heart, bearing the weight
of my sins in the Garden of Olives, and upon

the Crofs, was afflicted thereat; and griev'd
at the fight of my miferies; permit not your
grief and dolour., your precious blood, tears,
and fweat, to be unprofitable to me. Efficacioufly touch my heart , O my Saviour! however ungrateful and unworthy I am of your
love, you ceafe not to love me , you lov'd
me when I made no return , nay even when
I would not have you love me; but now fince
by your grace I have chang'd my mind grant
this my humble requeft : I give you my heart
dear Lord, and beg you to place me in yours,
make this the moment of my converfion, let
me begin to love you, and never ceafe to do
fo, let me be wholly confecrated to your love
as à perpetual flave, let me die to my felf,
that I may have no more life nor motion but
for you, and by you. Amen.

An honorable Amends to the Sacred heart of JESUS.

O Moft Adorable heart of my Divine Redeemer whom an infinite love has hid under
the Euchariftical fpecies, there to be our fouls
food , councel , fanctuary , confolation , and
all things elfe, penetrated as I am with grief
to. think of the blindnefs of Infidells , and ob-
tinacy of Heretics who will not acknowledge
you in this Sacrament of love, of the impiety

and facriledges of fo many bad Catholicks
who receive you in an ill ftate and dishonour
you fo many ways , of the negligence of fo
many remifs fouls who come to you without
preparation, without devotion, without hardly
any reflection, infine of the faults that I continually commit againft this Divine Sacrament,
I deteſt all thefe exceffes with my whole heart
and defire to make you an honorable Amends.

Pardon us O infinite fource of love, and to
make us more worthy of pardon, change our
hearts entirely. Grant that we may never approach you in an ill ftate , for human ends,
or for cuftom fake , nor ever, through negligence keep from you , but always come to
you with à pure confcience , à lively faith , à
right intention , an ardent charity, and à profound humility : grant us alfo O God of Goodnefs ! The happinefs to receive you worthily
at our death, that we may live of you , and
with you in à happy eternity. Amen.

Confecration of ones felf to the heart
of JESUS.

O Moſt amiable heart of my Divine Redeemer, I N. N. confidering your infinite love
for all men, and for me in particular, in view
of the oppreffing grief and other pains you
you have endur'd for my fins, in view of the

moſt Precious Blood you have been pleas'd
to shed for my redemption , in view of the
exceſſive love you have shew'd us in the inſtitution of the moſt Bleſſed Sacrament , and
in view of the infinite perfections, which makes you ſo amiable O heart of a God Man !
I this day conſecrate my ſelf unto you without
reſerve , for all the reſt of my life.

I conſecrate to you my body, my ſoul , my
thoughts, my deſires, my words , my actions,
and my ſufferings , deſiring thereby to contribute to your greater glory. In particular I
conſecrate to you my heart with all its motions, deſiring it may love you only , rejoice
in you only , and not breath but for-you alone,
and however unworthy the offering be , you
cannot refuſe it ſince you have ask'd it.

Receive it then O Divine Heart of J e s u s !
purifie it , ſanctifie it, enflame it with your
moſt pure love , ſo that it may not act but by
the motion of that love , nor ſuffer but for
your love , grieve only that it loves you ſo
little , have its only Joy in loving you much,
deſire nothing but the continual encreaſe of
that love , nor fear nothing but to let that
Holy love go out or relent; in à word, make
my heart like to you , that by you, with you,
and like you, it may eternally love the Father,
the Son , and the Holy Ghoſt. Amen.

A Prayer to obtain the converſion of hearts. -

O Divine heart of JESUS! which has an averſion for all iniquity, and ardently deſires the converſion of all ſinners, ſanctifie the hearts of all Mankind, give humility to all proud hearts; a love of poverty, and tenderneſs for the poor, to all avaritious hearts; a horrour of ſenſual pleaſures, and the love of purity, to all impure hearts; a facility in pardoning, and the love of enemies, to all revengeful hearts; make all hearts Holy as you are Holy; that they may be all pleaſing to the Eternal Father, and worthy temples of the Holy Ghoſt. Amen.

You may alſo in time of Salüe moſt profitably employ your time as follows.

AFter having ſaluted our Lord in this miſtery with all poſſible reſpect, unite your ſelf unto him, and to all his divine operations in the Holy Euchariſt : where he continually adores, praiſes, and loves his Eternal Father in the name of all men, and in the moſt perfect manner that can be imagin'd; that is to ſay in a ſtate of victim. Meditate and endeavour to conceive his recollection, his ſolitude, his hidden life, that admirable ſtripping himſelf of all, his obedience to the word

of any Prieft, his humility, and his other virtues, according to the model he gives thereof
in this Euchariftical ftate. Excite your felf to
imitate them, and purpofe to do it in occafions. But above all confider attentively the
admirable difpofitions of his heart in our favour, and all the fublime virtues it is the fource
of, the immenfe love he has for his Eternal
Father, his ardent charity for all men, and
eagernefs for their falvation. Endeavour to difcover in this Divine Heart, all thofe Abyffes
it contains, of humiliation, abaifement, poverty, fuffrance &c. Confider what are the fentiments of his Holy foul at the fight of mens
ingratitude, who treat him with fuch indifference : excite your felf to produce acts proper
to repair as much as may be, all thofe indignities by fentiments of gratitude, and principally by an ardent love for JESUS CHRIST.

Offer the Eternal Father his only Son JESUS
CHRIST, as the only victim worthy of him,
by which alone you can pay due homage to
his Soverain Majefty, acknowledge his benefits, fatisfie his juftice, and oblige his mercy
to fuccour you, fay to him with the Royal
Prophet : *Refpice in faciem Chrifti tui* look
on the face of thy Chrift. 'T is true my God
that I deferve to be treated as à rebellious
fervant, but Eternal Father! look on this dear
Son perfectly obedient, who at this moment

offers you himſelf on this Altar, the profoun'd
abaſements he is in, for the pardon of my infidelities and diſobedience : *Reſpice in faciem
Chriſti tui*, on whichever ſide your juſtice takes me, I will preſently offer this belov'd
Son to diſarm it : tho' I should à hundred times ſee your anger ready to break out upon
me, as many times would I repeat the ſame
thing *reſpice in faciem Chriſti tui.* I deſerve
nothing but I offer you à victim who merits
all ; and if he has not fully ſatisfi'd you, I
ever conſent to your refuſing me both the pardon of my ſins, and new graces : but you can
deny me nothing I ask in virtue of the merits
of JESUS CHRIST, in virtue of his ſufferings and
death, the reward of which is ours, ſince he
has made it over to us, grant me then in
virtue of thoſe Sacred ſufferings and preciour
death.

Here make your petitions and then go on.

I Ask à great deal, O Eternal Father ! but
I offer you the Body, the Blood, and the
Life of your belov'd Son Sacrific'd on this
Altar, as full payment for all I ask, what çan
I deſire ſo great, that comes not far short of
what I offer you for it ?

Offer your ſelf to God by the hands of JESUS
CHRIST, and Sacrifice to him your life, your
employments, your inclinations, your paſſions,

and in particular fome act of virtue that you
purpofe to do, or fome mortification that you
refolve to practice, and that for the fame ends
for which our Lord immolates himfelf in the
moft Bleffed Sacrament.

Offer your felf to JESUS to be ftraitly
united to him, begging him to let you enter
into his fpirit and fentiments, nay even into
his very heart, never more to go out of it;
then look on JESUS CHRIST as your head,
and confider your felf as his member, or elfe
as ally'd to him, as his fifter to whom he has
yeilded all his merits, and bequeath'd the re-
wards that his Father owes him for his labours and death. 'T is in this quality, as ally'd
to, or as members of the Eternal Word, that
we dare confidently appear before Almighty
God, treat as one may fay, familiarly with
him, and in fome fort oblige him to give us
à favourable audience, becaufe of the alliance
and union we have with his Son, and particularly through the infinit price, and dignity
of the victim we offer him in the moft Bleffed Sacrament.

Conclude with à fpiritual Communion accompany'd with à perfect confecration of all
you affections, and defires to the Sacred heart
of JESUS.

Or else you may may use this manner of Prayer.

AFter having made an act of faith and ador'd JESUS CHRIST in the Blessed Sacrament. Excite your self to love him tenderly, and beg him to enflame you daily more and more with his love. Then endeavour to enter into your self and to find out the state of your soul, simply discovering to your Saviour your faults, passions, weaknesses, infirmities, and the very bottom of all your miseries. Submit your self entirely to his Holy will, and equally bless him, for the chastisement of his Justice, and for the favours you receive from his mercy, Humble your self before his Soverain Majesty, make to him à sincere confession of your infidelities and sins : beg his pardon for them, and purpose to do better for the future.

Then enter as one may say, into the Adorable heart of JESUS CHRIST, consider what are his sentiments, how he contemns what the world esteems; what notions he has of those vain honours, of those seeming goods, of those fading pleasures, mixt with so much bitterness. At the same time consider what account he makes of that, which is disagreable to most people, how precious in his sight is à poor obscure life full of humiliation. Judge then

which muſt be in the right, either, we, who
ſo paſſionatly eſteem and love all that JESUS
deſpiſes, or JESUS himſelf who ſo forcibly
ſlights, and ſo expreſſly condemns what we ſo
eagerly ſeek for.

*This is à very profitable manner of Prayer
fit to disabuſe the mind and inſpire it with
that true wiſdom which we admire in the
Saints.*

*Receive the Bleſſing with all poſſible reſpeƈt
and devotion. And before you leave the Quire
adoring the Bleſſed Sacrament Say.*

Dear Lord I leave my heart in that Sacred
Tabernacle, and at your feet, there let me
live to love you, and die rather then offend you.

*Inſtruƈtions in order to viſiting the moſt
Bleſſed Sacrament.*

WHen we go to viſit our Lord in the moſt
Bleſſed Sacrament, we may behave our ſelves
as à perſon of quality would do when he goes
to court, to viſit his Prince : he may go.

Firſt to have the honour to ſee him, whence proceeds divers moſt excellent manners of
Prayers and aƈts, as admiration, eſteem, praiſe, benediƈtion, glorification, love, joy, con-
ſidering the infinit love our Lord expreſſes to
us in the moſt Bleſſed Sacrament, the extreme

defire he has to be with us, his meeknefs and
goodnefs. His marvellous care and more than
Paternal Providence over us , his liberality ,
his power, his wifdom, and his other perfections , which he difcovers fo refplendantly
in this Divine Miftery. Remark the heroick
examples of Humility, Obedience , Patience ,
and other Virtues , which he gives us therein, upon which we may make divers affections of the will, according to the nature of
thofe perfections, and draw from thofe examples efficacious conclufions for the regulating
of our lives.

Secondly to render homage to his Majefty ,
which we may do to the infinite Majefty of
this God Man , and that as to our Soverain
Lord, our natural Prince, our true God , our
Creator, our Confervor, and our All : believing, acknowledging and owning him for fuch.
And from this follows two moft noble Manners of Prayer : firft by way of interiour and
exteriour Adoration ; the fecond by way of
Offer, offering all to him , as all is his and
comes from him.

Thirdly to thank him for his graces ,and
benefits , Innumerable are thofe we have receiv'd both fpiritual and corporal ; but we
ought never to omit returning him our moft
grateful thanks , for that he has been pleas'd
for the love of us, to reduce himfelf to fuch

à state in the Blessed Sacrament; for all the wonders he works therein, and for all the Blessings, he thereby bestows upon us.

Fourthly, to expose his necessities, let us humbly and filially represent ours unto him, and beg à remedy. Ah! if we knew how to make à right use of the treasure we have in the Blessed Sacrament, we should not be so miserable as we are.

Fifthly, we may visit our Lord to enjoy his divine presence in repose and union of spirit, staying and reposing in him as in our center. And also to practice the exercise of love, producing all sorts of acts thereof; which must necessarily be most ardent, being animated with the presence of their object.

Sixthly, we may go to our Lord like Nicodemus to have our doubts clear'd; Like Magdalen to beg pardon for our sins; Like the Centurion to obtain the cure of à sick servant; Like the Leper to be cleans'd of our sinful leprosy; Like the Deaf and Dumb to get speech and hearing; Like the Prince of the Synagogue, who begg'd him to restore life to his only daughter just dead.

Seventhly, we may go to our Lord in the same spirit, that the poor goes to à liberal rich man; the hungry to à magnificent banquet; the thirsty to à clear fountain; the disciple to his master; the friend to his dear friend; the afflicted to his comfort; and the cold perfon to à Good fire.

But as you have not now the liberty to go to the Bleſſed Sacrament when ever you pleaſe, and may hereafter be in à country where you cannot do it, you may at leaſt go thither in ſpirit and deſire : imitating therein the Holy Prophet Daniel; who three times à day opening his chamber window which look'd towards Jeruſalem, kneel'd down, and entering in ſpirit into the Holy Temple, ador'd God as he us'd to do, when he aſſiſted there in perſon at the Sacrifices.

Nothing can be oppos'd againſt ſo eaſie à practiſe of piety, ſince only your mind and heart need be employ'd in theſe ſort of viſits, and your exteriour occupations need not be long interrupted, ſince one moment is ſufficient ; neither need you fear being obſerv'd, ſince your viſit will paſs in the ſecret of your heart. You will offer to God the Sacrifice of praiſe according to the advice of the Pſalmiſt, but your heart will ſerve for an Altar in theſe occaſions : neverthelefs it may be ſaid for your comfort, that you will not gain leſs, nor will JESUS hold himſelf leſs honour'd thereby, when you cannot viſit him otherways.

When then you may not, or cannot go before the moſt Bleſſed Sacrament, to viſit the Son of God, go in deſire; and turning to the fide where you know he repofes, fay the fame things, that you would fay at the foot of his Altars; and you will merit as much, and will not pleafe him lefs, than if in effect you were there to adore him.

Prayers, and Acts of Devotion proper for the hour of Adoration before the moft Bleffed Sacrament.

ALl Affociates of this devotion ought to Communicate on the day, wherein their hour of adoration falls, and befides the affign'd hour, they should be careful to fpend well and devoutly the three days of shrovetide, beftowing at leaft an hour (either all together or at feveral times) before the Bleffed Sacrament: as alfo on the feaft of the Bleffed Sacrament, with all the days of the Octave, and one of the two fundays following, and when it is expos'd. Each alfo should be careful often to make thefe fallowing afpirations, at leaft on the Eve and day of their hour.

O Good JESUS! hear I befeech you the Prayers that are offer'd for me, and grant me à happy death.

Prais'd be for ever the moft Bleffed Sacrament of the Altar.

JESUS be for ever ador'd, blefs'd, and lov'd in the moft Bleffed Sacrament of the Altar.

The

The Preparatory Prayer.

COme O Holy Ghoft ! replenish my heart
with thy grace, and enkindle in it the Sacred fire of thy love; that I may render to
JESUS in the moſt Bleſſed Euchariſt an honour, that may be pleaſing and acceptable to
his Divine Majeſty, in imitation of thoſe Blef-
ſed Spirits, who inceſſantly adore you in heaven. Grant that I may make a reparation according to my power for all the injuries you
daily receive from infidells, Heretics, and
bad Catholicks. Infuſe your ſeven gifts into
my ſoul to purify every thought of my mind,
and affection of my heart, that I may think
on nothing but JESUS immolated on our Altars for the love of us poor miſerable ſinners.
Grant I may not be diverted by any voluntary or involuntary diftraction during this
my time of Prayer, and adoration all which
I deteſt and difavow; befeeching you O Queen
of heaven, and Bleſſed Saints of God, to obtain for me a participation of that fervour and
devotion, wherewith you ador'd this amiable Miftery, that in union of your Holy difpoſitions, I may adore my Saviour in this
Sacrament, in the moſt perfect manner I am
capable off, that ſo my Adoration may be acceptable to his Divine Majeſty, to the glory
of his Name, and profit of the whole Church.

G

Bleffed Angels and happy Saints of Paradife, I moft humbly beg you to praife, blefs,
glorify, adore and give thanks, to my Soverain Lord, and Saviour JESUS, in my behalf,
give him I befeech you, all that honour I
am oblig'd to render his Divine Majefty, and
I with my whole heart and affections, humbly unite and Join my intention to all the
Love, Adoration, and Glory you shall ever
give to this Sacred and Adorable Sacrament,
even to the end of ages, and the long extent
of a whole eternity.

Prais'd be for ever the moft Bleffed Sacrament.

May JESUS be for ever ador'd in the moft
Bleffed Sacrament.

*Then if you cannot meditate, you may
make ufe of the Prayers and devotions mark'd
for* Salüe, *page* 78. *if you can meditate, here
follows à very proper Meditation.*

MEDITATION.

I. POINT.

COnfider firft, what muft have been the fentiments of the heart of JESUS forefeeing the
number of injuries, and outrages he was to
endure in the moft Bleffed Sacrament from
the malice of hereticks even to the end of
ages. There is nothing more fenfible to a ge-

nerous heart than ingratitude, especially when,
it is attended with the utmost contempt : But
the blackest ingratitude of all, is that, by
which benefits are not only unrequited, but
even deny'd to have been receiv'd, thereby
to have all liberty to misuse the benefactor
without seeming to act like the ungrateful.
J e s u s then distinctly knew that at certain
times there would be great numbers of Christians, who would unmercifully renew upon
his Sacred Body in the Adorable Eucharist,
all the outrages that the malice of devils could
be capable off, and who, that they might
have all freedom to exercise their fury and
rage upon him, would push their malice to
such an excess, as to deny the real presence
in the Blessed Sacrament.

Who would ever have thought men capable of so black a malice : or who can ever
imagin a more afflicting contempt, than to
see the most resplendent mark of the most excessive love ; made use off, to injure the lover most excessively? J e s u s foresaw all that
has happen'd in these latter times. He saw his
Temples prophan'd, his Altars demolish'd,
his Priests butcher'd, and his Adorable Body
dragg'd upon the ground, trod under foot,
and become an object of scorn and insolence
to the most profligate wretches, and of horror
and execration to the ungodly.

What muft have been the fentiments of the tender and generous heart of JESUS, at this fight ? Ah Dear Lord ! muft you then work fo great à miracle to furnish men with à means to ufe you fo unworthily? Muft you thro' an excefs of love remain with them to the end of ages, that you may be as long the objeet of their contempt and rage ? Sure fuch a fight is fufficient to make à heart wither away with fadnefs and grief. Is it you then O King of glory ! that I fee in fo many places loaded with opprobries and ignominies? Is it you O God of Majefty ! before whom the Seraphins fink down with refpeet, that I fee fo infolently treated by poor miferable worms? Infine is it you, O Objeet of the Eternal Fathers delights, who are become an objeet of horror and execration to your creatures, your flaves, nay your own children, and all becaufe you have lov'd them to much?

Lord, could one have ever imagin'd an ex- cefs of malice in men anfwerable to the excefs of your Goodnefs ; an excefs of ingratitude correfpondent as one may fay , to the excefs of love with which you have lov'd us?

But my amiable Saviour! shall I not even exceed this excefs of ingratitude , if confide- ring the fentiments you muft needs have had at the fight of thefe cruel ingratitudes , I am my felf infenfible of your pain?

'T is here Lord, that you seem to me like what your Prophet has painted you : *noviſſimum virorum*, *virum dolorum*, the heretics have treated you as the laſt, and moſt deſpis'd of men, nay they have fulfill'd the Prophecy which declar'd you ſhould be ſatiated with opprobries. But, my God, ſhall thoſe hereticks, thoſe unnatural children, thoſe ungodly wretches, be never ſatisfied with uſing you ſo inſolently, nor ſhall I never be touch'd at the ſight of your ill uſage?

This fatal image, this diſmal view, caſt you into à bloody ſweat : grant it may at leaſt move me to tears, and if my heart cannot feel the ſame grief which oppreſs'd yours, let the ſhame of being ſo inſenſible of your pains, ſupply in ſome ſort for my inſenſibility.

SECOND POINT.

COnſider ſecondly, it was an object no leſs ſad and afflicting for our Saviour, to ſee the ingratitude of moſt of the faithful themſelves, who would be ſo cold, indifferent and even forgetful of him. This amiable JESUS then ſaw the ſmall eſteem, nay the apparent contempt they would have of the greateſt proof of his moſt ardent love. He ſaw that whatever he had done to be belov'd by, and to be continually with the faithful, in inſtituting the Adorable Euchariſt, they would not be engag'd to love him, nor even hinder'd from forgetting him, neither by thofe excefles of love, his benefits, nor by his very prefence.

He reprefented to himfelf thofe Churches where he refides for the moft part without adorers; and the difrefpect and immodeft comportment of his people when they were in his prefence. He diftinctly faw all thofe many Catholicks who lofing whole hours in vain amufements, or unprofitable vifits, who fpending moft part of their time in idlenefs, can never find leifure, or to fay better, are hardly ever in the humour to pafs a quarter of an hour at the feet of his Altars, infine they cannot refolve to vifit him, and fcarce adore him once à week after their cold manner. He knew how many others would vifit him without devotion, and how many irreverences they would commit in thofe vifits, and infine, how few would ftrive to make their court unto him. This amiable Saviour clearly perceiv'd that moft would no more mind him. Than if he where not upon earth, or than if being upon earth, he were not what he is in heaven.

The ill ufage, hard heartednefs, and contempts of the Jews, gentils, and heretics, were à moft fenfible fight unto him, but infine they are his declar'd enemies, and what better can be expected from an enemy? But to have thofe who own and acknowledge his be-

nefits, that little flock which makes profeffion
of being faithful to him, nay even his own
children, to have them I fay, be infenfible
of his benefits, and unmov'd at the grief fuch
fights caufe him; nay even flight him themfelves in their turns, muft have been to this
dear Saviour an affliction above human com-
prehenfion. Ah! How well might this Divine
J e s u s fay, if the Pagans, the Turks, the
ungodly by profeffion, had utter'd injuries
againft me, I had fuffer'd them without com-
plaint. *Si inimicus meus maledixiffet mihi*
fuftinuiffem utique. But that Chriftians, that
Catholicks, whofe Redeemer I have not only
been, but whofe food I daily am, nay that
my own children should treat me with fuch
indifference and contempt! *Tu verò homo*
unanimis qui fimul mecum dulces capiebas
cibos!

At this view, at this difmal thought what
were the fentiments of the heart of J e s u s?
That is to fay, of the moft generous, the moft
tender heart that ever was, a heart paffionate
for the hearts of men, which he found cold,
hard, and refifting.

Super omnes inimicos meos, fays he by his
Prophet, *Factus fum opprobrium.* It had not
been much to have been the May-game and
fable of my enemies, if at leaft in the midft
of thofe opprobries, I had found many fer-

vants and faithful friends, but alas! 'T is quite the contrary.

Qui videbant me foras fugerunt à me. They have no sooner seen me difguis'd by love un- der the weak appearences of bread, that I might have the pleafure of being with men, but they kept ftill à greater diftance from me : They forfook me and forgot me, as à perfon who had no place in their heart. *Oblivioni datus fum tamquam mortuus à corde.*

Ah Dear Lord! I think of all this, and at the fame time refleft that it is à God, who freely accepts and fuffers thefe opprobries, and torments for me, without dying with grief or love?

If a man, if a flave, had endur'd the hund- reth part of what JESUS has endur'd, and do's daily endure upon our Altars for the love of us, we could not forbear loving him, having a gratitude for him, and giving him at leaft fome marks of compaffion : muft then JESUS crucify'd and dying for us, JESUS daily for- gotten, defpis'd, mifus'd for the love of us in the Adorable Eucharift, be the only per- fon whofe pains and love we are infenfible of, and whom alone we requite with coldnefs and ingratitude? What hardnefs? What infenfi- bility? Is the heart of man capable of fuch an excefs.

Alas Lord! it is but too capable of it, and

(105)

will but too much make it apparent, if the same love that obliges you to expose your self to so many indignities and outrages for ungrateful man, do's not also oblige you to soften the hardness, and warm the coldness of his heart, to render it sensible of your outrages, and susceptible of your love. For alas! all the wonders you have work'd, and torments you have sufferd, will but serve to harden me, and render me more criminal; if I am neither mov'd at them, grateful for them, nor love you the better.

But my God, as I hope you will not refuse me your grace, I from this moment make strong resolutions of giving you for the future most certain proofs of my love and just acknowledgment, I have indeed been insensible of your benefits, and sufferings; and behav'd my self with indifference towards you, notwithstanding my knowledge of your continual presence with us. Therefore have I great reason, my amiable Saviour, to mistrust my fair resolutions and promises having been till now so inconstant and unfaithful in your service. But methinks your mercy inspires me now with more courage, and gives me hopes that I shall for the future be more constant, and faithful to the promise I make you, of endeavouring by my respect in your presence, my frequent visits, and my assiduous making

court to you, to teſtify my ſincere devotion
to your Sacred heart, and the ardent deſire I
have of doing what poſſibly I can in the remainder of my days, to repair by my love,
my reſpect, and by all ſorts of homages, all
the contempts and outrages you have ſuffer'd
in the Adorable Euchariſt; as well as the for-
getfulneſs and ſtrange indifference that moſt
have for your adorable perſon, in the moſt
Bleſſed Sacrament of the Altar.

PRAYERS WHICH SHOULD NEVER BE OMITTED
IN THE HOUR OF ADORATION.

Firſt for ſuch as are in the ſtate of grace.

M Y God, I conjure you by your infinite
mercy, to pitty my miſeries, reſtore me that
Juſtice and ſanctity which I loſt by ſinning,
and hear from your Holy Sanctuary the petitions I offer for all aſſociates of this perpetual Adoration who happily are in the ſtate
of grace : I beſeech you by the merits of your
Precious Blood, grant them the grace of à
happy perſeverance, and increaſe of your love
till the end of their lives, for which effect accept of thoſe prayers in union of all the Holy
diſpoſitions which the Saints have had in reciting them.

Pater, Ave, Gloria Patri.

Secondly for all such as are in
mortal sin.

MOst Dear Redeemer, I humbly befeech
you, look favourably upon all aſſociates of
this perpetual Adoration, eſpecially on all
thoſe who are in mortal ſin; I conjure you
by the blood you shed for them on the croſs,
and love you have had for them from all eternity: grant them remiſſion of all their ſins,
and the true ſpirit of penance, that they may
be converted to you by à ſincere amendment
of there lives, loving and ſerving you to the
end, and ſo eternally ſing your mercies in the
company of Saints and Angels; for which
effeɕt I humbly offer theſe petitions, in union
of all the intentions and diſpoſitions of Holy
ſouls.

Pater, Ave, Gloria Patri.

Thirdly for all thoſe who are in
death's agony.

O Dear Saviour JESUS! I humbly implore
your mercy for all aſſociates, of this perpetual Adoration, that are now in their laſt con-
flicts, and death's agony: deny them not
your powerful grace, make them triumphant
over their enemies, grant them perſeverance
in the Catholick Faith, and belief of your

divine Mifteries, with a Holy fear and love,
and all difpofitions neceffary to die the death
of the Juft, that they may eternally continue
their Adoration ; for which intention I offer
thefe prayers , uniting them to the love you
had for your Eternal Father , when you taught
your difciples to pray in this manner.

Pater, Ave, Gloria Patri.

Fourthly for all the affociates in
Purgatory.

DEar Lord, I befeech you have mercy on
the fouls of the affociates of this perpetual
Adoration, who are now detain'd in the rigorous flames of Purgatory, grant them eternal reft, let your glorious light shine on them,
admit thofe once members of your miftical
Body upon earth, to be now united to the
members of your glorious Body in heaven :
accept in fatisfaction for their fins the infinite
merits of your bitter death, and paffion, which
I offer for them; remember my God you redeem'd them with the price of your deareft
blood , which I adore in this Sacrament :
and that I may offer fome fatisfaction for
them, accept thefe Prayers in union of all the
love, that is pay'd you in heaven or on earth.

Pater, Ave, Gloria Patri.

*Fifthly for the neceffities of the Church,
and converfion of infidels.*

O God of infinite Goodnefs, receive favourably the humble petitions I addrefs to you
in this divine Sacrament, for all the neeeffi-
ties of your Holy Church, that all may have
grace to ferve you faithfully, each one in
their degree and function : convert all infidels
to the Chriftian Catholick Faith : grant that
all Heretics and Scifmaticks, laying down
their errors may enter into the bofom of the
Roman Church : let all the wicked and im-
pious be converted from their bad lives, that
all unanimoufly may honour you in this Sacred Eucharift : O that this admirable Adoration were not only perpetual, but univer-
fally and generally practis'd throughout the
whole world as it is in heaven : and as you
are your felf in à continual Act of Adoration,
and love towards your Eternal Father! O divine JESUS ! to obtain the effect of all thefe
things as far as your infinite wifdom knows is
to be to your greater honour and glory, I
unite my intention to the intentions of all good
and virtuous fouls in thefe Prayers.

Pater, Ave, Gloria Patri.

An Act of Contrition, and spiritual Communion.

O My Lord JESUS CHRIST, true God, and true Man, my Creator and Redeemer, for your own infinite Goodnefs, and becaufe I love you above all things, I am heartily forry I have offended you, and purpofe firmly by the affiftance of your grace, never to offend you more, to fly all occafions of evil, humbly to confefs my fins, and faithfully to do penance the reft of my life : I confidently hope in your mercy to obtain à full remiffion of my fins, which I beg by the merits of your death and paffion, grant me the grace of an efficacious amendment, and perfeverance in your love to my laft breath, O my dear Saviour ! let me now at leaft receive you fpiritually into my heart, come then my dear JESUS, the love of my foul, come dear Lord, annihilate and deftroy all my paffions and vicious inclinations : eftablish in my heart the Empire of your love, enthrone your felf there as a Soverain : replenish my foul with your graces, that I may ever be acceptable in your divine fight, intimately united to all your wills and affections, live you in me, and I in you ; and never permit me to be feparated from you by any voluntary offence : grant me grace to ferve you faithfully in this world, that dying the death of the Juft, I

may bleſs, praiſe, and glorify you with the
Saints and Angels for all eternity.

A Prayer to our Angel Guardian.

B Leſſed Angel, my deareſt and faithful
Guardian; you who always ſee the face of
God in the poſſeſſion of eternal glory, better
know than we poor mortals, what reſpect and
veneration my Saviour J E S U S merits in this
Divine Sacrament : you know my obligations,
and have ſeen the many defects I have committed during the hour of my Adoration. I
am a poor pupil committed to your charge and
care, act now the part of a true and faithful
friend, pay my debts for me, ſupply my defects, I am unable to acquit my ſelf, you my
reſpondant, anſwer then for me; and ſince I
cannot always be employ'd in an actual Adoration of my JESUS in the Bleſſed Sacrament,
praiſe, bleſs, thank, & adore him for me : I
unite all my affections to all the praiſes, benedictions, and thanksgivings, which you
Bleſſed Angel conjointly with all the other
heavenly Citizens, render to my God in this
Sacred Miſtery; and hope your charity, will
obtain à bleſſing for me, all this family, and
all our friends and kindred; obtain us alſo
grace in this world to praiſe, bleſs, and adore
him, who lives for ever and ever, and ſing

to him everlaftingly together with you Sanctus &c.

Prais'd, Ador'd, and Lov'd, be for ever
the moft Bleffed Sacrament of the Altar.

A MANNER
OF
SAYING THE ROSARY,
PROPER FOR THE HOUR OF PERPETUAL ROSARY.

*Offer the firft five Tens for fuch as are in
mortal fin, or any neceffity either fpiritual
or temporal.*

*In the firft Ten addrefs your felf to our Bleffed
Lady as fhe is daughter of the Eternal Father, reflect on her fingular priviledge, con-
gratulate with her for all the prerogatives
of Joy and blifs fhe enjoys under this title,
give thanks for the favours receiv'd by her
means, and at the end of the Ten add à*
Gloria Patri, *and this afpiration.*

ASPIRATION.

O Sacred Virgin! moft dearly belov'd daughter of the Eternal Father, employ your credit, and powerful interceffion for all your
servants

servants, and associates who unhappily are fallen by sin from the right of filiation, and are become children of satan; mercifully reclaim them I beseech you.

AT THE II. TEN.

Consider our Blessed Lady, as she is Mother of the Eternal Word: make the same reflexions as before.

ASPIRATION.

MOnstra te esse Matrem; shew your self a Mother, especially to poor sinners; obtain them mercy of your Blessed Son, and restoration of grace; by the merits of his bleeding wounds I beg it.

AT THE III. TEN.

Consider our Lady, as she is Spouse of the Holy Ghost, &c.

ASPIRATION.

SAcred Spouse of the Holy Ghost, comfort your desolate servants and associates in their distresses: rouse them from their tepid languors, by the fire of your charity; enflame them in your ardours, O Mother of love!

H

AT THE IV. TEN.

Confider our Lady as the Temple of the Bleſſed Trinity, &c.

ASPIRATION.

O Sacred Temple of the living God! reſtore this title to your ſervants, that by ſin have loſt it : ſtrengthen thoſe that are tempted to forfeit it, and never permit them to become ſlaves of the devil, by tranſgreſſing the laws of God.

AT THE V. TEN.

Confider our Lady as Queen of Angels, and Men, &c.

ASPIRATION.

O Sacred Queen! caſt à favourable eye on your poor ſubjects here on earth, eſpecially thoſe that have devoted themſelves to your ſervice in this Roſary; and have compaſſion I beſeech you particularly on thoſe, that are in any affliction ſpiritual or corporal,

*Offer the second five Tens for the Agonizing;
and confider five of the chief Virtues most
resplendent in our Ladies life ; making Acts
of love, complaifance, and admiration, and
defiring to imitate, as well as admire.*

AT THE I. TEN.

Reflect on her ardent love.

ASPIRATION.

O Mother of beautiful love ! if ever you
imparted any fparks of your divine fire to
any of your fuppliants, we now humbly beg
that favour for all your Agonizing affociates;
that they may happily die of love , and
live eternally to love , and praife Almighty
God for ever.

AT THE II. TEN.

Confider her profound humility.

ASPIRATION.

O Sacred Virgin , Mother and Miftrefs of
the humble ! fuccour your Children Agonizing, and ending their courfe of this mortal pilgrimage ; obtain them a profound humility, that they may attain to eternal Salvation.

AT THE IIL. TEN.

Confider her Virginal Purity of Soul and Body.

ASPIRATION.

O Virgin of Virgins! have compaſſion on the ſouls of your Agonizing Servants, that are terrifi'd with the apprehenſion of paſt offences, where with they have unhappily defil'd their purity of Body and Mind; obtain them true contrition and eternal life.

AT THE IV. TEN.

Confider her firm hope, and Confidence in God.

ASPIRATION.

O Mother of the deſolate! obtain à firm hope and confidence in the mercies of God, for all the Agonizing of this Confraternity; take from them all diffidence, and obtain them eternal reſt.

AT THE V. TEN.

Confider her Heroical patience.

ASPIRATION.

O Mother of the miſerable! comfort your afflicted Agonizing Servants; obtain them true patience in their ſufferings, and à happy paſſage to an eternity of joy.

*Offer the third five Tens for the associates
in Purgatory.*

At the I. Ten.

*Consider our Lady as your Mother; and give
thanks for all her tender love, and Motherly care of you, &c.*

ASPIRATION.

O Dearest Mother! distill the milk of your
mercies on the poor souls suffering in Purgatory; consider them as your children, and let
your mercies be to them a heavenly dew to
mitigate their flames.

At the II. Ten.

*Look on the B. Virgin as your Lady and
Mistress; give thanks for all favours receiv'd from her under this title; look on
your self as her servant and handmaid.*

ASPIRATION.

O Dearest Lady! employ your credit with
your Son for your suffering servants in Purgatory, cover and hide their faults under the
mantle of your charity.

AT THE III. TEN.

Look on the Blessed Virgin as your Protectress, give thanks for all favours of Protection.

ASPIRATION.

O Sacred Virgin! you are our refuge : cast à favourable eye on your afflicted Clients in Purgatory ; appease the Divine Justice in their behalf; present these our small devotions offer'd for them, and render them effectual for their succour.

AT THE IV. TEN.

Look on the Blessed Virgin as your Advocatress, give thanks for all favours obtain'd by her intercession.

ASPIRATION.

O Sacred Virgin, prove now à powerful Advocatress for the poor souls suffering in Purgatory, obtain them à speedy delivrance.

AT THE V. TEN.

Look on the Blessed Virgin as à dear and confident Friend, give thanks for all favours in that nature.

ASPIRATION.

O Glorious Virgin! offer these prayers to

your Bleſſed Son, for your Friends, and
ſervants ſuffering in Purgatory; grant they
may be effectual for the delivrance of ſome
of them.

*When you have done your Roſary, if the
hour be not yet expir'd, you may devoutly
recite our Ladies Litanies, or ſome other
Prayer in her honour; and frequently in
the day time, make this ſhort petition, or
aſpiration to our Lady.*

O Sacred Virgin, gracioufly hear the Prayers
which are continually offer'd for me.

When it thunders you may ſay.

† Chriſtus vincit, † Chriſtus regnat,
† Chriſtus imperat.

JESUS, MARIA, ANNA, JOSEPH.

Fortitudo mea Domine, firmamentum meum,
Deus meus, & liberator meus.

℣. Adjuva nos Chriſte, & libera nos.

℟. Propter nomen tuum dulciſſimum Jesu.

℣. Et Verbum Caro factum eſt.

℟. Et habitavit in nobis. Amen.

*A Prayer to obtain the grace of à happy
choice, as to à ſtate of life.*

I Adore O my God! that Divine providence, by which you diſtribute proper gifts to

all, and chufe each to embrace the ftate, in
which you defign to operate his falvation.

I firmly believe that in your Eternal pre-
fcience, I am predeftinated to embrace à ftate
hitherto known to you alone.

And that which difquiets me O God of
mercy! is, to reflect that there is no fecurity
for me in any ftate, but in that which you
have eternally defign'd me, and yet that ftate
is unknown to me.

In this uncertainty O Eternal Wifdom!
proftrate before your throne of Majefty, I do
pour out my heart in your prefence. For who
can attain to the knowledge of the incomprehenfible fecrets of Divine Providence? Or who
can certainly know what God requires of him?
The thoughts of mortal Men are fleeting and
uncertain : they can hardly comprehend what
paffes here on earth, and what they fee
with their own eyes. Who then can found
heavenly things? Or who, O great God!
can know your defigns, unlefs you give him
wifdom, imparting your Holy fpirit from the
higheft heaven?

Speak then my God, for your fervant
hearts.

Enlighten me with the light of your truth,
and thereby conduct me to the ftate you call
me too.

Let me know the way I should walk in, becaufe I keep my foul, elevated to you.

Teach me to do your wil, for you are my God : in you I place all my confidence, through JESUS CHRIST, our Mediator, and your only Son. Amen.

⚜❖✦✦✦✦✦✦✦✦✦✦✦❖⚜

That you may even in this life reap the fweet fruits of an Eternal glory , accuftom your felf to make frequent acts of love, as for example.

M Y God I delight in you; I wish you dear Lord , all the glory you can receive from creatures.

I love you my God , more than all that is not your felf.

Dear Lord , let me rather die à thoufand times than difpleafe you.

Ah that I could die for the love of you my God!

O God of my heart ! you are all love ; enflame my heart with the fame.

Let me die my Saviour, that I may fee you.

I grieve my God to fee you fo little known, honour'd, and lov'd, and fo much offended.

O my Sovereign Lord ! may your will be done on earth as it is in heaven.

All this I mean dear Lord , as often as I shall fay, *my God I love you with all me heart.*

IN ADVENT.

It being the Churches defign in the inflitu-
tion of this Holy time, that grateful thanks
should be render'd to God for the Incarnation
of his Divine Son; purpofe never to pafs à
day without acquitting your felf of that duty:
and to exprefs your defire of that Defir'd of
all nations, make frequently this afpiration.

O JESUS my Saviour and my God! haf-
ten to poffefs my heart, and never more forfake it.

Your chief intentions during this Holy time
ought to be.

1. To honour the Eternal Word, and his
Holy Humanity.

2. To honour the Bleffed Virgin, Mother
of the Adorable Word Incarnate.

3. To prepare the ways for the fpiritual coming of JESUS into your heart.

Adore then, and ferve the Word who is
coming to you. Honour the Virgin, and implore her interceffion, by whom he is given
unto you. And endeavour to fanctifie your felf
the better to receive that Divine Saviour.

IN LENT.

Confidering this Holy time as given you by
God to think continually of the Paffion, and
Death of his Divine Son; let that be the

*ferious fubject of your Meditations : and en-
deavour to render your fafting more meritorious and fruitful, by offering each week for
fome good end, and pious intention.*

OFfer the firft four days to obtain grace to
begin, purfue, and finish this Holy time for
the glory of God, and your own falvation.

Offer the firft week, in thanksgiving for all
benefits.

The fecond, in fatisfaction for your fins,
and the converfion of finners.

The third, for all the neceffities of the
Holy Church, in particular thofe of the family
you live in.

The fourth, for the fouls in Purgatory, and
confolation of the afflicted.

The fifth, for thofe you are oblig'd to pray for.

In Holy week redouble your fervour; to
do, and fuffer as much as your ftrength, and
fuperiours will permit.

Upon Good Friday, make an honourable
Amends to Jesus Crucifi'd; begging pardon
for your fins, and offering him your falts; befeeching him to apply efficacioufly the fruits
of his paffion to your foul.

*Each day of Lent being a day of falvation
for you, endeavour daily to perform the following things.*

1. Go to mafs as to Mount Calvary, there

(124)

to ſee, and adore JESUS Crucifi'd, under the vail of the Holy Hoſt.

2. Suffer ſome little hunger, cold, or the like; uniting your pains to thoſe of JESUS ſuffering.

3. Be exact in your faſt, and abſtain from ſome particular ſin, or fault.

4. If you can hear ſermons, never fail to do it; and pray for all Preachers, that God would pleaſe by their diſcourſes to touch the hearts of their auditors, and always convert ſome.

5. Adore our Saviours five wounds, ſaying devoutly at each, à *Pater* and *Ave*, or ſome other proper Prayer.

Three days preparation for Holy Communion, very proper to prepare for the firſt Communion, and à not leſs profitable preparation for any other, if you have time and devotion.

ONe of the moſt important things in à ſpiritual life, is certainly, the uſe of the moſt Bleſſed Sacrament: for the Sacraments operate, and communicate grace according to the diſpoſitions of the receivers; ſo that often one shall receive more grace from God and ad-

*vance farther in the way of virtue by one
only Communion, than another shall do by
fifty. Therefore it is moſt ſoverainly important to thoſe, who would advance in virtue,
and acquire perfection, to diſpoſe themſelves
well for this great Miſtery; remembering that
it is not ſufficient to communicate, but to
communicate well.*

*In order to which, behold here a moſt ex-
cellent manner of preparing to receive that
God of Majeſty.*

THE FIRST DAY.

*Endeavour to conceive well theſe
three things.*

1. Who it is that comes to your heart.
2. For what end he comes.
3. And what he brings with him : and then
draw ſuitable affections, which makes the preparation.

I. CONSIDERATION.

WHo is it that comes? 'T is our Lord
JESUS CHRIST, true God and true Man,
our Father, our Brother, the Spouſe of our
ſouls, our Protector, our Comforter, our perfect Friend, our Phyſician, our firſt beginning, our laſt end and beatitude, our Joy and
our all.

II. CONSIDERATION.

FOr *what end do's he come?* O the end is
most admirable ! He comes to communicate
his Divinity to each Man in particular, for he
could only do it to one in the incarnation;
this amourous Miſtery extends it ſelf to all,
ſince God realy, and perſonally, enters into
all, communicates and unites himſelf to all
that receive him. Behold then the end of this
Sacrament of love.

1. To produce the union of God infinitly
loving, with Men infinitly beloy'd, for love
is à virtue uniting the lover with the belov'd.

2. And by that union to apply to Man who
receives him, efficaciouſly and abundantly,
the merits of his life and death, and to enrich him with his treaſures, ſanctify his body
and ſoul, and conſecrate them as à Sacrifice
to his Eternal Father, as his own body and
ſoul have been; to make him proportionably
live à Divine life like his, and imprint in him
an effective ſeed of the beatitude he is one day
to poſſeſs.

He enters man with an immortal and glorious Body, not mortal and paſſible as that
was which he offer'd his Eternal Father on
the Croſs, that he may communicate by the
union of that Sacred Body, endow'd with im-
paſſibility, clarity, ſubtility, and agility, to
the Body and ſoul of Man, à certain inpaſſi-

bility againſt ſin, à clarity, à ſubtility, and
an agility to produce well the moſt Heroical
acts of all virtues, and give them à moſt ſtrong,
and ſweet aſſurance of their future glory.

III. Consideration.

Hat do's he bring with him? He brings
grace, beauty, light, the joy of infinite treaſures, and infine all the bleſſings that the
union of God with Man can cauſe : who, as
the Apoſtle ſays, becomes thereby the ſame
ſpirit with God, and proportionably like; as
the humanity of our Lord became by the union
it had with the perſon of the Word.

*After each of theſe conſiderations produce
the following acts.*

Act of Faith.

Es I believe that I shall receive this glorious, this luminous, this miraculous Body,
Soverainly beautiful and perfectly amiable;
that I shall receive thoſe all-healing hands,
which by à touch cur'd ſo many ſick; thoſe
charming eyes, which with their looks have
converted ſo many ſinners; that moſt Holy
Soul, the greateſt of all the wonders of God,
and next to God, the moſt worthy object of
the beatitude and Divinity; nay I shall receive the moſt Bleſſed Trinity with all its per-

fections. I believe all this; I believe my God is there, and that I shall possess all these treasures.

ACT OF HOPE.

What Blessings then may I not hope from this visit, and most desirable possession? I hope that those medicinal hands will touch and cure all my wounds; that those benign eyes will behold me with mercy and pity, and that, that divine mouth which never open'd to condemn any, will say to me words of comfort, of benediction, of grace, and of life. I hope that his most Holy Soul will sanctify my soul; that his memory will fortify my memory; that his understanding will enlighten mine; and that his will all enflam'd with the love he bears me, and so charmingly testif'd by this visit, will enflame my will with his love. Yes believing what he is, and the ends for which he comes to me, I can do no less, than hope in his goodness and love for all this, and much more.

ACT OF JOY.

O What reason have I to rejoyce? What happy cause have I for an inexplicable content and Jubilation of heart, to possess the Son of God, his Body, his Soul, his Divinity and do possess him in himself, so intimately,

and

and for fuch defirable effects ? Come then, O come my hearts defire! both my body and Soul wish for you with all poffible affection. O come my God! my heart expects you.

After which, moft ardently wish and defire his coming : firft for your own intereft, that you may poffefs all thefe bleffings ; fecondly and much more, in confideration of God himfelf, to procure the moft Bleffed Trinity, the Sovereign glory he receives thereby. Here you may frame the moft pure, and fublime intentions that can be made; to wit, that you communicate to glorify Almighty God, to pleafe him, to render the merits of Chrift efficatious; uniting your Communion with that, which it is thought he made at the laft fupper communicating himfelf. Or elfe you may offer it for the remiffion of your fins ; to gain fome virtue, or to overcome fome vice, &c.

But if you believe, hope, rejoice, and defire ; you ought not lefs to reverence this great God, and humble your felf in his prefence : believing for certain that he is the omnipotent God, the Creator, and Preferver of heaven and earth, the King of Kings, and Lord of Lords ; before whofe infinite grandeur and Majefty, the Angels, the Cherubins, and Seraphins tremble with refpect, and the greateft Monarchs are as if they were not : on this

I

account, make fervent interiour acts of reve-
rence, abasement, and annihilation, and both
interiour, and exteriour acts of humility.

THE SECOND DAY.

I. CONSIDERATION.

COnfider ferioufly the ftrange and admirable manners of our Lords being in this Divine Sacrament, and coming to us.

That at the fimple word of the Prieft, at the very moment it is pronounc'd, he defcends from heaven to earth, and places himfelf in the Hoft, thus punctually, and without delay, obeying the voice of à wretched Man, who very often is his mortall ennemy.

II. CONSIDERATION.

JESUS is under the Sacramental fpecies in à moft furprifing manner, in abaifment, fweet-nefs, love and goodnefs, which ravishes all the Bleffed fpirits with admiration and won-der. He puts his infinite greatnefs and Ma-jefty, under the fpecies of bread and wine; he therein places his Divinity with his good-nefs, his beauty, his wifdom, his power, and all his perfections.

He is there in the moft noble and precious union, that the Divine Wifdom ever inven-ted; which is the hypoftatical union of the Divine Word with human nature.

He puts herein the fineſt creature that is amongſt pure ſpirits, to wit, his own moſt Holy Soul; before whoſe beauty, goodneſs, ſanctity, wiſdom, grace, and glory, the moſt perfect Cherubins, and Seraphins, appear but as ſtars before the ſun.

He alſo puts therein his own Sacred Body, which is the moſt beautiful, and moſt compleat that has ever been, or ever ſhall be amongſt Men, together with the immenſe ſplendor it receives from the union of ſuch à Soul, and much more from that of the Divinity : the veins and arteries of which, are full of the precious blood, with which he has waſh'd away all the ſins of the world.

All this he puts under theſe ſpecies ; and hides under ſo poor à cover, and under the accidents of ſuch trivial and common creatures as are bread and wine, all the ſplendor of his Divinity, and glorify'd Humanity. O what an exceſs of abaiſment and love.

And what ſtill raiſes this exceſs yet more is, that he puts, and reduces himſelf entirely not only in the whole hoſt, but even in each particle of it, ſhrinking, ſtraitning, and as it were annihilating himſelf for the love of Man : and for his love, on the other ſide, multiplying, and putting himſelf as it were, in each Hoſt as many times, as there are parts and particles of it ; ſince he is there all entire, and all in each part thereby dearly teſtifying to Man, the extream love he bears him, and the infinite defire he has to communicate, and unite himfelf unto him.

III. CONSIDERATION.

COnfider moreover the prodigious miracles that God works in this Sacrament, and how he turns nature upfide down to come to us : for his body is in heaven and upon earth; and being à true fenfible, vifible, and palpable body, he places, and holds it under the Hoſt, infenfibly, invifibly, impalpably, in à fpiritual manner; he deſtroys the fubſtance of bread and wine, conferves their accidents without fupport ; gives them the force to nourish, as if it were their fubſtance, befides other moſt miraculous operations.

IV. CONSIDERATION.

ANd that which goes beyond all that can be thought, or faid is, that tho' God be the Sovereign Majeſty, and infinite purity, who mortally hates impurity and fin; yct he had rather fuffer à thoufand irreverences, and pafs thro' the foul, filthy, and impure hands of à wicked Prieſt, than deprive one foul of the content and good of receiving him; fo great is his defire of communicating and uniting

himſelf to Man, and ſo extreme is the love
he bears him.

ACTS OF THE WILL.

1. *Of admiration for ſuch an extremity of
affection.* Certainly, if Faith did not teach us
theſe things, we could never belive them; for
tho' we may have read, or heard of many
admirable inventions of love, found out by
Men madly paſſionate, or even charm'd and
bewitch'd : tho' we caſt our eyes on all the
Poëts fictions, who have ſpent themſelves, and
drain'd their wits in diſcribing à perfect and
exceſſive love : yet all that together (ſuppo-
ſing it were true) all thoſe ardours, thoſe
langours, thoſe charms, thoſe artifices, and
metamorphoſies do not come near the leaſt
part of what is done in this Divine Sacrament.
O God! what marvels For à God to deſcend
from his throne, and come from heaven to earth,
and there hide, and cover his infinite ſplendor,
and Sovereign Majeſty under the vile accidents
of bread and wine? To ſhrink up, reduce,
and as it were annihilate himſelf to à point
for me? To break down all the laws of nature, and do ſeven or eight great and ſtupen-
dious miracles for the love of me? O what
wonders! what ſubject of moſt raviſhing admiration! how true is it my God, that having
lov'd Men, you lov'd them particularly at the

end of your live, eſtablishing for them this Adorable and Divine miſtery.

2. *Of Soverain love for ſuch à love, and of deſires moſt enflam'd of uniting your ſelf to this God of love.* Theſe muſt be lively animated, and often reiterated, being mixt in proper places with acts of an Appreciative love : proteſting that before all creatures of the univerſe, you hold him for the only object of your heart and affections; that you will prefer him before the whole world, before your ſelf, your Body, your Soul, your goods, your honour, and your life, adding thereto affective offers of them all.

3. *Of Hope firm and aſſur'd.* That ſince our Lord do's ſuch ſtrange things to come to us, to unite himſelf to us, and to communicate his infinite bleſſings and treaſures unto us; his coming will certainly produce its effect, if we diſpoſe our ſelves as we ought.

IMITATION.

Since God do's ſo many ſtrange, and wonderful things to come unto me; 'tis ſurely but reaſonable that I on my ſide, do great things alſo to go unto him : he obeys, he abaſes himſelf, he makes himſelf little, he ſuffers indignities, and overturns nature for the love of me; I likewiſe, to ſhew, and love him with a mutual love, will to day, particularly, and perfectly practice obedience, abasement, mortification, overthrowing and stifling in my self all the motions of corrupt nature; infine I will bring all possible dispofitions; to prepare my self for this Divine visit.

THE THIRD DAY.

AFter having briefly confider'd who it is that comes, as on the first day : reflect attentively what you are, and whither you go; considering not only your nothing, ignorance, miseries, and corruption, but alfo your past fins, which renders you unworthy of all graces, and by confequence of that of Communion which is infinite; moreover your prefent fins and imperfections, your want of difpofitions, the fmall purity, humility, love, and fervour which you render to this miftery; comparing what you are, what you do, and what you give to our Lord, with what he do's to come to you, and what he brings you with him.

ACTS TO BE PRODUC'D.

*Of a profound reverence, and excessive humi-
lity, springing from the comparison of our
Lord with your self. Here say, and repeat
with the humble Centuron, Domine non sum
dignus &c. with the following explications.*

ACT OF HUMILITY.

O My God! I am infinitly unworthy to approach you, and receive your infinite Majesty,
because of my nothing, of my most great and
innumerable sins, of the little service I have
render'd you, of the small love I bear you,
of my want of à perfect purity, and in general, of my want of dispositions to receive you :
therefore knocking my breast, I say from the
bottom bottom of my heart, *Lord, I am not
worthy &c.*

ANOTHER ACT OF HUMILITY.

A Nd because, tho' I should have the love
of the Seraphins, and should render you as
many services as your Saints have ever done,
and will do for eternity; and tho' I had all
the dispositions, all the sanctity, all the purity, and humility of Angels and Men, and
even of all possible creatures : yet should I be
infinitly unworthy, and indispos'd to receive
you worthily, therefore I again repeat; *Lord,*

I am not worthy that thou should'ft enter under my roof, fay only the word, and my foul shall be heal'd.

Another Act of Humility.

Since then I am fo uuworthy to receive you, and fo far from deferving it; I befeech and conjure you by that Soverain Sanctity, purity, and Majefty, which is in you, and requires fovereign difpofitions; that being in me as you are in all creatures, you would pleafe to receive your felf in me and for me; and by the infinite purity, fanctity, love, and perfection that you have in me, to receive your felf according to your merits, and fo fupply for my impurity, coldnefs in love, indignity, and all my indifpofitions : to which intent I à third time fay; *Lord, I am not worthy &c.*

Then excite your felf to à cordial Contrition for your fins : it being more than reafonable to be moft heartily forry for the leaft offence committed againft à God fo great, fo good, fo fweet, fo amiable, fo obliging, and fo liberal.

And to à tender, fincere, and perfect Love. Confidering that being fo vile and unworthy as you are, and he fo great, and full of glory, yet that infinite inequality do's not hinder him from teftifying an enflam'd defire to come unto you, and in effect to come with à fingular

Sweetnefs, and incomparable love. O incomprehenfible, and infinite love of God! O excefs of unmeafurable charity! That which would never enter the mind of an earthly Prince who is but à Man, à frail veffel of clay, is practic'd daily by the God of the univerfe, when he comes from heaven to earth, and brings himfelf, not by the miniftry of Angels (which would have been à very great favour) but by his own hands, the moft precious, and exquifite meat that the heavenly banquet affords, to wit, his own Sacred Body, Soul, and Divinity; and this to à poor miferable creature, who is here below as in à true hofpital, needy and fick.

After the Acts of love, should follow ardent defires of this vifit from your God and hopes to receive the bleffings his hands are full off.

❖❖❖❖❖❖❖❖❖❖

The Teftament of à perfon devoted to the moft Bleffed Virgin, to conftitute her the Heirefs of all she is, and has.

MOft Bleffed, and moft Sacred Mother of my God: J. N. N. being in my right fenfes, and mov'd by the love I bear you, (tho moft unworthy of your amiable prefence) freely

take and chofe you for my Lady, and univerfal heirefs of all the good I have ever done,
faid, thought, or endur'd, either interiourly
or exteriourly; and of all the good that I do,
or shall ever do, fay, think, or endure : of
which I make over to you an irrevocable do-
nation, taking from my felf all power to an-
null, or leffen it by any other difpofition whatever.

I conftitute you alfo the Lady, and Miftrefs
of my foul and body, of my heart, of my life,
and particularly of my death; at which I moft
humbly befeech you, O moft dear Mother,
to affift, for to have care of all I shall do,
as belonging to you in quality of my Heirefs.

I moft humbly befeech you, Dear Lady,
with all the extent of my affection, to prefent
your dear Son with this little unworthy inhe-
retitance which I offer you, to the end he
vouchfafe for the love of you to like, accept,
and put it into the priviledg'd dominion of his
infinite goodnefs and merty : and I affure my
felf that if you pleafe to favour me with this
grace, that he will accept it from you as à
moft precious treafure, tho' it be lefs in value
and merit, than the widows mite mention'd
in the Gofpel : this I hope from your goodnefs; deny not à poor finner, the moft miferable of thofe who by their disloyalty have
exafperated your moft amiable Son.

(140)

O Sacred Quires of Angels, and you Blessed Saints of Paradise, but particularly you who have been favorits to the Lady I now constitute for my universal Legate, I take you all for witnesses of this my disposition, and most humbly conjure you to assist me at the general, and particular Judgment against my enemies, in case they have any pretention to my works, or thoughts; all which I have offer'd, consecrated, and given irrevocably to the Mother of my God: and in the mean time obtain for that ill manager my Soul, who has so much wasted the goods and favours she has receiv'd from God, à perfect contrition for all her offences; add the grace to be such in life and death, as the Divine Goodness desires.

Obtain me also I beseech you, all the Holy virtues requisite for my perfection, and for the augmentation of the Blessed Virgins inheritance; to whom I protest, and take you for witnesses, that if I could encrease this her possession with as many good works, acts of faith, confidence, love, gratitude, and all sorts of virtues, as there are stars in the sky, grains of sand in the sea, atoms in the air, animated, and inanimated creatures which have been, are, and shall be to the consummation of the world, or which might be produc'd during à whole eternity, I would do it with

all my heart; and esteem my labour most happy
for so perfect, and accomplish à Lady and
Miftrefs. This is my will declar'd by word of
mouth, and sign'd in prefence of heaven and
earth, the   of   in the
year   N. N.

*Chufe fome folemnity of our Lady to make
this Teftament upon, that of our Lady of
Nives is very proper: and 'tis good to renew
it on all our Ladies feafts after Communion;
and at the hour of death, defiring to have
it bury'd with you.*

A Manner of combating, and overcoming à vice.

First, perfwade your felf firmly that you
have à great many vices and faults; becaufe
nature having been fpoil'd, and corrupted
by Adams fin, there can be nothing in our
fouls or bodies which is not vitiated.

Without this perfuafion à perfon remains
blind in the knowledge of her vices and imperfections, grows old in them, and carries
them to the grave; nay she even becomes fo
nice and delicate in the matter, that she cannot hear of them without being angry: whereas
when she do's not doubt of this verity, she

keeps her felf with great humility in the fight
of God , and is difpos'd to find out her failings , to learn them from others, and then
to correct them. Now in order to fight, and
overcome à particular vice, obferve what follows.

I.

You muft know it well, and weigh the hurt
it do's you, and the Good it deprives you of:
how it is à fource of daily pains and falls,
which you entertain; and not getting rid of it,
you nourrifh in your bofom an Afp and dra-
gon, which will fting you, and fooner or later
be your death.

I I.

After confidering the evils that this vice
caufes, and will furely caufe you, if you do
not take an order with it : endeavour to conceive à hatred and horrour thereof; and make
à fix'd refolution to fet upon it , and deftroy
it, whatever it cofts you.

I I I.

To which intent you ought to ftrike at the
root; that is to fay, kill it in your will by
averfion and hatred, for there it lives by the
fecret affection you bear it. Few undertake
the battle , and victory over their vices
as they should do , therefore with all their
pains they feldom compafs the matter : they

pass them slightly over, and labour only to
correct some of their defects, but never go
to the source of the evil. Now as 'tis the soul
that is that source, and in that the vice is
conceiv'd, form'd, and lives in the will; so
tis in the soul, and in the will it should die;
and as the love we bear it, and the pleasure
it gives, makes it live there, so the contrary
which is hatred ought to be the death of it.

I V.

Take care diligently to avoid the occasion
of falling into this vice, and if you meet with
any, keep firm and be faithful to our Lord,
who has thus dispos'd things for to give you
the means to destroy this vice, and to draw
from you a proof of the love you have for
him.

V.

If you happen to fall, rise again swiftly,
without being angry, or fretting at your self;
beg pardon for your fault, and impose some
penance as well to correct that fault, as to
make your nature wiser for the future.

V I.

Do every day some interiour, and exteriour
actions of the virtue contrary to that vice.

V I I.

Consider how our Saviour has practis'd that
virtue, that you may imitate him.

V I I I.

Let your lectures be on that subject, to in-
struct you.

I X.

Refer your Prayers, your Communions,
and all your exercifes of piety to this defign.
viz. To obtain the victory over that vice, and
gain the oppofite virtue.

And by à particular examen, fee each day,
the progrefs you make therein.

OF A PARTICULAR DEVOTION.

*IT is moft advantagious for every one to
chufe, and take to heart fome one or more,
fpecial object of praife, or devotion, fince
we shall not read the life of any Saint, nor
the converfion of any finner, whom Gods
particular mercy fav'd, but that we shall
find they ow'd thofe fignal bleffings to fuch
à particular devotion, and their conftant perfeverance in it.*

TAKE THESE FOR EXAMPLES.

1. TO JESUS in the Bleffed Sacrament. 2. To
JESUS Crucify'd and dying on the Crofs for
you. 3. To the Holy Ghoft, the love and
mercy of God. 4. To God the Father; whofe
power creates all, whofe liberality beftows all,
whofe providence difpofes of all. 5. To our
Bleffed

Bleffed Lady the Mother of mercy. 6. To the heart of JESUS. 7. To fome particular Saint. 8. To your Angel Guardian. 9. To JESUS his infancy, chiefly in the manger. 10. To JESUS his private life with MARY and JOSEPH in the houfe of Loretto at Nazareth. 11. To, and for the fouls in Purgatory. 12. To the Bleffed Trinity, the infinit power, unlimited wifdom, Eternal love.

Some one of thefe devotions being chofen, the duties by which it may be practic'd are many, and extremely conducing to true and tender devotion. As for example. 1. Get fome book that treats of the miftery, or Saints life that is the object of your particular devotion, read it ofton, endeavour to retain what you have read, and whenever you can, read fuch. 2. Take all occafions to fpeak of fome paffage of that miftery, or of that Saints life. 3. Have à picture thereof at your Oratory; and if pof- fible, carry à little one about you to look upon often, and kifs. 4. Have fome proper Prayers to addrefs to it at different times of the day. 5. Offer all your good actions, or fufferings as Sacrifices, in honour of that mif- tery, or by the hands of that Saint; or (if that be your devotion) for the fouls in Pur- gatory. 6. In all little afflictions comfort your felf with the object of your devotion; in all comfortable news or occurrences, acquaint him

as the author of it, or mediator that obtain'd
it : in all doubts consult him : in all fears
make recourse to him. 7. Set aside one day
in the week, or at least in the month to honour him particularly by all sorts of duties, as
Communion and Mass in his honour, some spe-
cial Office or Prayer, some Alms, or Charitable Actions, rehearsing something of him in
conversation, &c. 8. At the beginning of each
lasting action offer it to him, or by his hand;
do it as if were in his company, remembering
something of him in like actions, if it be à
Saint, or our Saviour, or our Lady. 9. Particularly when you observe any troublesome
temptation, or any ailement or pain, entertain
your self with him amorously, and confidently
about it.

*Many such practices will be suggested to
à true spiritual love ; but above all, whatever
you begin, be sure to persevere, for therein
consists the whole merit.*

A most easie means to solace the poor Souls.

MY God, I offer you all the infinit satis-
factions of the passion of your only Son, and
all those of your Saints; I desire to Join with
them as much as I can, all that shall be sa-
tisfactory in the good you shall grant me the

grace to do this day; and with all my heart
I offer it for the fouls in Purgatory.

Receive it I befeech you my God, in fatisfaction for the pains of fuch à foul, or of many,
(according to your devotion or obligation.)

OF THE ANGELUS.

*Say it at night in honour of the incarnation
of the Son of God.*

AT the firſt *Ave Maria*, thank almighty
God, for having choſe ſo admirable à means
to fave Mankind. At the ſecond, rejoice that
ſhe has choſen the Holy, and happy Daughter of Joachim, to be his worthy and well belov'd Mother. At the third, beg JESUS and
MARY to give you à Holy life, and happy
death.

*Say it at noon in honour of the paſſion, and
death of JESUS upon the Crofs.*

AT the firſt *Ave*, thank our Saviour, that
he would ſuffer for our Salvation the ignomi-
nious death of the Crofs.

At the ſecond, honour the Bleſſed Virgin
by the Crofs of her Son, and compaſſionate
the diſtreſſes of her motherly heart.

At the third, beg our Saviour to give you
his Mother to be yours, as he did to S. John;
to the end that ſhe take your life and death
under her ſingular protection.

Say it in the morning in honour of our
Saviours Refurrection.

AT the firft *Ave*, Adore JESUS rifen, and
thank him for having taken poffeffion of im-
mortality and glory for himfelf and you.

At the fecond, rejoice for the incredible yoy
that the Bleffed Virgin had, when her Divine
Son came to vifit her after his Refurrection.

At the third, beg JESUS and MARY to
keep you in the joy of à goqd confcience,
both in life and death.

Remember Chriſtian Soul that you
have to day.

A God to love and Glorify
A JESUS to imitate.
A Mother of God to honour,
All the Angels to invoke.
All the Saints to pray to,
A Body to mortify.
A Soul to fave.
Virtues to beg.
Sins to expiate.
A Heaven to gain.
A Hell to avoid.
An Eternity to meditate.
A Time to manage.

A Neighbour to edify.
A World to apprehend,
Devils to fight with.
Paſſions to quell.
Perhaps à death to ſuffer.
And à Judgment to ſuſtain.
Think well on it.

Brief Practices to ſolemniʒe the principal Feaſts of the year.

HAving prepar'd your ſelf during the Advent, to receive an incarnate God into the crib of your ſoul.

At Chriſtmaſs.

REceive him with all the honour, affection, admiration, humility, &c. which you can poſſibily produce.

At the firſt Maſs, honour the eternal Birth of the Divine Word in the boſom of his Father, and ſalute him as your Saviour.

At the ſecond, honour his temporal birth of the Bleſſed Virgin, and ſalute him as your brother.

At the third, honour his ſpiritual birth in your ſoul by means of his holy grace, and ſalute him as your King.

At the Circumcifion.

Give Jesus your heart for à new-years gift :
and confecrate to his glory, all your thoughts,
words, and actions of the enfuing year : then
thank him for the firft effufion of his blood,
which he pours out for the falvation of finners.

At Twelve - tide. -

Offer him all the faculties and powers of
your foul, with the Mifterious prefents of the
Mages, and pay him the homages of your liberty.

At the Purification.

Beg of the Bleffed Virgin à communicati-
tion of her purity ; that you may make her
Son à moft pure, and agreeable offering of
all you have left.

At Shrove - tyde.

Say this following prayer 350. times, to repair the injuries, and affronts then offer'd to
the infinite Majefty of God : our Lord himfelf
taught it to Ste. Mectilda for that intent.

To thee be praife, to thee be glory, to thee
given thanks in the world of eternity, for all the
injuries & affronts done unto thee by thy members us wicked finners. Amen.

In Lent, as page 120.

At Eafter.

USe all your endeavours, after having fuffer'd with JESUS CHRIST, to rife again
with him by his grace ; and to rejoice with
the whole Church for the glory of his Refurrection.

At the Afcenfion.

FOllow your Saviour to heaven in thought;
and conjure him, fince you cannot actually
follow him, not to leave you an orphan upon
earth; but to fulfill his promifes of à comforter : to obtain which blefling, frequently repeat during the ten following days this short
Prayer.

O Come Holy Ghoft ! replenish &c.

On Wit Sunday.

IMplore graces with the Blefled Virgin, and
the Apoftles, by their interceffion, and by the
fuffrage of the Church.

On Trinity Sunday.

ENgulf, and lofe your felf in the thought of
this Adorable Miftery ; and offer him each
moment your acts of praife, and thanksgiving.

On Corpus Chrifti.

SOlemnife the triumph of JESUS with all
poffible devotion ; by frequent affiduities at

the foot of his Altars , by continual Adoration , and thanksgiving for the inftitution of
this Auguft Sacrament , by which he gives
and unites himfelf to us.

On the Affumption.

REjoice with the Angels for the glory of
the Bleffed Virgin : beleech her to be your
Advocate in heaven ; to the end that having
imitated her virtues , you may partake of the
happinefs she enjoys.

At the Nativity of the Bleffed Virgin.

MAke the fame prayer to her , and beg the
grace never to pafs à day without rendring
her fome fpecial fervice , and remitting to her
conduct all your affairs , defigns , and enter-
prifes.

At the Feafts of all Saints.

UNite your praifes with thofe of the Bleffed
and beg the fuccour of their Prayers , that
you may be one day eternally reunited with
them in heaven.

On all Souls day.

SPend the whole day in Prayers for the folace of the faithful departed , both for your
Parents and Friends , and for all others who

have more need of affiftance. In the mean
time think ferioufly of your laft end, and difpofe of the affairs of your confcience as if you
were certainly to die prefently after, and be
put into the ground; which thought alone if
well made ufe off, will be enough to withdraw
your foul from all occafions of fins.

A MEDITATION

*To enter into the difpofitions of making
à happy death.*

Place your felf in the prefence of God.
Befeech him to infpire you.

*F*Or *à foundation to this Meditation you
muft well conceive this truth, that life is only
lent us by God : therefore if we are not always ready, and difpos'd to reftore it to
him again, we refufe him the right of fovereignty over our being.* All men are once to
die , and then be Judg'd , *fays the great
Apoftle.*

*So confidering this verity that we are to
die but once, and that an ill death cannot
be repair'd in à whole eternity ; let us fee
how neceffary it is for us not to be furpris'd,
but to be always upon the watch like the
fervant who expeas the coming of his mafter.*

I. POINT.

NOW since we must necessarily die, 'tis of great importance for us to comprehend this verity : that death being most certain , and the hour most uncertain , all Christian wisdom consists in preparing our selves well for it ; which is indeed to us the affair of affairs , and the sole and only busipess we have to do in this world ; since we are here only to save our souls , and losing it we lose all : *for what will it profit à Man to gain the whole world if he lose his own soul?* Says our Sovereign master JESUS CHRIST.

O God ! how great is the blindness of most Men , who not thinking of this divine verity , live à terrestrial , sensual and animal life , never raising their mind to celestial things ; but so strongly fix their affections to this mortal life , that they prefer it to the Eternal one? *He that loves his life*, says our Lord, *shall lose it, and he that hates it in this world, shall gain it for eternity.*

O my God ! 'tis not then to love ones life well, for to have too much attach to it, since that attach to the temporal life , proceeding from an irregular love of our selves, puts us in danger of losing the Eternal one, and you assure me, that *he who comes not to you and hates his life, cannot be your disciple.* Give me then dear Lord, à Holy hatred of this

mortal life, which may make me continually
tend, and pretend to the Eternal one, to love
you world without end. Amen.

II. POINT.

PRecious in the fight of God, is the death
of his Saints, fays the Pfalmift. Now if we
would die like Saints we muft live like Saints;
always keeping our affections as difengag'd
from earthly things, as if we were to die each
moment, fince there is no moment in which
we may not be fupris'd by death, and in
which we ought not to be difpos'd and prepar'd to receive it, except we will hazard our
falvation : alfo furmounting the natural fear
we have of death, by the faith and confidence that JESUS CHRIST who keeps the keys
of life and death, and loves us infinitly more
than we love our felves, will fend it to us at
the time, and in the manner, he has in his
providence forefeen to be beft for us. Has he
not created us for Eternal life? Do we not
believe it more happy than this mortal life?
If thefe are not our fentiments we have no
faith, and by confequence no hope, fince we
cannot arrive to that Bleffed life he has promis'd us, but by death; and what charity can
à felfifh foul have, who loves her life more
than the will of her God, and fears more to
die, than she defires to fee him, and be uni-

ted to him? *Perfect charity.* Says the scrip-
ture, *expells fear.* And if we ought to shew
our love to God, by our hatred to fin, how
do we hate it fince knowing we cannot live
without committing it, we ftill fear death fo
much? O if we had à true love, with what
joy should we embrace it! that we might be
in à ftate of no more offending his infinite
goodnefs, fince the fmalleft fin, as Divines
teach, is much more to be dreaded than death
it felf.

III. Point.

IF God should give us the choice of the time, hour, and manner of our death, could
we order it better than he do's by his infinite
wifdom, power, and goodnefs, he who having made us for himfelf, and redeem'd us
with his precious blood, defires nothing fo
much as to fave us, and make us attain to
our end? And fince Faith teaches us this verity, why do we not entirely abandon to him
the care of our life and death? What can there
be better for us in heaven, on earth, in life,
and in death, than to accomplish his moft
Juft and Holy will? And feeing we muft ne-
ceffarily undergo the orders of it, is it not
better to do it meritoriously by an humble
fubmiffion and filial confidence in the Divine
goodnefs, than to execute it by force as the
devils do, and by our refiftance render our

action more worthy of chaſtiſement than of re‑
ward? If the fear of our ſins makes us appre‑
hend death, and deſire life to do penance in
it; what better penance can we do, or more
pleaſing to God, than to conform our ſelves
perfectly to his will, and undergo, the decree
of our death, to render him the obedience
à creature owes to its Creator, and witneſs
that we prefer the honour of pleaſing him be‑
fore our own life? If acts are eſteem'd meri‑
torious proportionably to the difficulty of their
execution, what can be harder to us than to
renounce our life? And what better penance
can we do, than to give it freely to God,
ſince in that gift we not only give him all
that we can give him, but alſo all that is
moſt dear unto us? *No man hath greater cha‑*
rity than to give his life for his Friend, ſays
our divine Saviour. And if à God has been
pleas'd to die à dolorous, and ignominous
death for us, and give his life upon à Croſs
for our ſalvation, shall we dare to refuge him
ours? Do we eſteem our life more precious,
or more neceſſary than his? O my ſoul! if we
have any love for God, or gratitude for this
Sovereign benefit, ought we not to wish we
had à thouſand lives to give him? What have
we which do's not belong to him? O my God!
ſince I am nothing but by you, I will be no‑
thing but for you, and provided I am what

you would have me be, 't is no great matter whether I live or die.

AFFECTION AND RESOLUTIONS.

SInce my Eternal Salvation depends on the moment of my death, grant me the grace my God, that by à true hatred of fin, à perfect contempt of the world, its vain honours, pleafures, and riches, and an entire renouncement of my felf, I keep my felf always prepar'd for that laft hour, and never fleep in the forgetfulnefs of death; for fear that letting the lamp of charity go out, and wanting the oil of good works in my foul, you should furprife me in that condition, and fay to me as to the foolish Virgins thefe dreadful words, *I know you not:* grant then dear Lord that I ever expect your coming, and deferve to enter with you to the eternal nuptials, *where eye has not feen, nor ear heard, nor the heart of man conceiv'd, what you have prepar'd for thofe that love you.* Give me my God the light of your Holy fpirit, that I may not be deceiv'd, nor feduc'd by my fenfes, taking the falfe for the true; and let me not efteem the things of this life good or bad, but as far as they draw me near, or divert me from this end.

(159)

CONCLUSION.

LEt us conclude this Meditation with this verity, that if we would die the death of the Juſt, we muſt live the life of the Juſt; ſince the true means to obtain a happy death, is to lead a good life: and as there is nothing more precious, nor more deſirable than a happy death, ſo there is nothing more deplorable, nor more dreadful, than an unhappy death; and the beſt means to ſecure us in an affair of ſuch importance, is to live each day, as if we were to die at the end of it, keeping ever our affections as diſengag'd from earthly things, as if we were at the point of death, in which al that is not God, will ſeem but ſmoak unto us.

A MOST
PROFITABLE EXERCISE,
TO PREPARE FOR DEATH.

A momento mortis pendet Æternitas.

On the day when you ſhall make this exerciſe, at your awaking enter into the thoughts of death, and look on that day as the laſt of your life.

I. POINT.

IMagin your ſelf on your death bed, and that your good Angel comes to you from God, to announce the irrevocable doom of your death , and says to you as Isai did to Eze-chias. *Dispose of your affairs, for you shall die and not live.*

Prostrate at the foot of your Crucifix or before the Blessed Sacrament , implore from the bottom of your heart, grace and light of the Holy Ghost, assistance and succour of the Blessed Virgin, your Patrons, and your good Angel, then make the following acts.

Act of Resignation.

1. MY heart is ready my God, my heart is ready, not my will but yours be done in me, with me and by me, now and for eternity.

O Eternal immense, and infinite God ! you suffice your self and have no need of your creatures : what matter whether I live or die, so I do but accomplish your Holy will in which alone consists my true life? Let it not be then my God, as I will, but as you please.

Confession of our nothing.

2. FOr to aknowledge the dependance I have, on you my Sovereign Creator, and to plainly confess before heaven and earth that you alone are, and I wretched creature am not; I embrace with an humble submission the destruction of this corruptible being, and consent that by

death

death it return to the nothing from whence
you drew it.

Reftoration of our being to God.

3. O My Sovereign Creator! I will reftore
you the being you have given me; and for
that effect, I accept of death in the manner
which shall moft pleafe and glorify you; difpofe then of your creature, and deftroy this
body of fin, in punishment of the offences it
has committed againft your Majefty : let the
earth return to earth, but let the fpirit created
to your image and likenefs, return to your
Divine bofom.

Acknowledgment of God's fovereignty.

4. O My good God! tho' my death be neceffary, for your love, I will render it voluntary, and rejoice that it will put me in à ftate
of no more refifting the Sovereign power, that
as lawfull Lord of all creatures you have over
me : I accept it in punishment of my misufe
of the free will you have given me.

To receive death in chaftifment for fin.

5. SInce death O my God! is the chaftife-
ment you have ordain'd for fin; with an hum-
bled and fubmiffive heart to your moft Juft
decree, I accept it in fpirit of penance, with
L

all the pains, humiliations, and privations
which follow it, in satisfaction for all those I
have committed.

Offering of our life to God.

6. O My Saviour! receive the Sacrifice I
make to your Divine Majesty, of my body
and life, which I offer you, and immolate as
à victime and Holocaust: unite it with that
you offer'd for me on the Cross, and consum-
mate it by the fire of your Divine love.

Desire to render to JESUS CHRIST
death for death.

O My Divine JESUS! since the love you
bear me, made you die on à Cross for my
salvation, 't is but reasonable that for you, I
freely accept of death, in exchange as much
as I can, for that you have endur'd for me.
O that I had à thousand lives to give you for
that effect, and to testify that you are my God!

SPIRITUAL CONFESSION.

With profound humility at the feet of JESUS
CHRIST, as if he were present to you in his
Holy Humanity, accuse your self to him, of
all your sins by à brief review, but especially
of the most notable ones: after which excite
your Soul to à lively and amorous repentance.

' *Act of Contrition.*

O My God ! proftrate before your Sovereign Majefty, I moft humbly beg pardon for
my great contempt and abufe of your Holy
graces, and for all the fins I have committed
fince my birth, in thoughts, words, and deeds;
I retract and difavow them with all my heart :
yes my God, with all my heart I retract them,
renounce them, and wish I had never committed, them; not for the pains they deferve,
but only becaufe I have offended your infinite
goodnefs, which merits to be infinitly lov'd,
and ferv'd by all creatures. O why is my
heart not capable of an infinite grief to efface
them ? But accept O my God, to fupply for
what I want, of that which my Saviour had
in the garden of Olives and on the Crofs, for
all the fins of the world, and mine in particular : accept likewife for the fame effect, the
forrow and contrition of all your Saints :
cleanfe me from my hidden fins, and pardon
me thofe I have committed by others : defpife
not my God, an humble and contrite heart,
which only hopes pardon from your fole mercy,
which mov'd you to fay, that when the finner should lament, you would no more remember all his iniquities.

And if you are pleas'd my God to continue
my life, I make à firm purpofe of amendment
with your Holy grace, efpecially of fuch,

and fuch, faults. And to endeavour to repair
the paft.

*Having finish'd this act, receive the abfo-
lution that JESUS CHRIST the Sovereign
Prieß gives you, by applying to you his Divine merits: then hear him fay to you as to
Saint Mary Magdalen, thy fins are forgiven
thee, go in peace.*

Say the 5o. Pfalm Miferere *in fpirit of
penance.*

Afpirations to the three Divine Perfons.

O Eternal Father! fince you have fo lov'd
the world as to have given to it your only
Son; I hope falvation from your mercy, feeing
you did not give him to condemn but to fave
us, and to that effect impos'd on him the moft
fweet name of JESUS.

O Divine JESUS! be to me à JESUS, remember that you faid you were not come for
the Juft but finners. O my God! you will not
the death of à finner, but that he be converted, and live, convert me then to you that I
may live an Eternal life.

Come Divine Spirit, repofe in my foul with
your feven gifts, to purify, vivify, juftify,
and fanctify it. Confume by the fire of your
love, all that's earthly in it, and fortify it
in this laft paffage againft all the temptations
of its enemies.

ACT OF FAITH.

1. I Proteſt my God before heaven and earth, that I will die in the faith and union of the Holy Catholick, Apoſtolick, and Roman Church, that I firmly believe, all it believes and teaches, becauſe you my God, Eternal verity, have ſaid or reveal'd it, and that you are an infinite goodneſs and ſanctity which cannot deceive, an infinite wiſdom which cannot err, and omnipotence it ſelf. I now diſavow all the temptations, and contrary ſuggeſtions, that my enemy may ſuggeſt to me at the laſt moments of my life, and moſt humbly thank you my God for the great favour you have done me in admitting me to the number of the children of your Holy Church.

Recite the creed, reflecting upon each article, and proteſting that you believe them all.

ACT OF HOPE.

2. O My God! tho' for the inconceivabe enormity and multitude of my ſins, I moſt Juſtly deſerve hell; yet confiding entirely in the merits of my Saviour, and in the infinite greatneſs of your mercy which can pardon more than I can commit, I ceaſe not to hope for the remiſſion of them, and the grace of

a Holy perfeverance in your love, to which
I efpecially confecrate the laſt moment of
my life.

ACT OF CHARITY.

3. DEar Lord, when shall my foul be feparated from this mortal body, and all creatures, and be perfectly united to you, and love
you with that pure and unchangeable love,
with which your Bleſſed in heaven love you?

What would I have in heaven or on earth,
but you, the God of my heart, my God, and
my Eternal portion.

I have eſteem'd all things as filth and or-
dure, to gain JESUS CHRIST.

Act of the love of our Neighbour.

4. MY Sovereign Lord, I beg grace and
falvation for all the creatures that you have
redeem'd with your precious blood, efpecially
for the children of your Holy Church, and in
particular for thofe who have given me any
difpleafure, whom I forgive, my God, for the
love of you, as I defire you should forgive me.

Defire to receive JESUS CHRIST.

5. O My God, my Creator, and my Redeemer! my beginning, and my end : my only
fatiety and beatitude : I have an extreme de-

fire to receive you, that I may be united to
you Come then to my foul I befeech you,
fanctify it, and replenish all its powers; come
to my body, and purify all its fenfes; come to
my heart and poffefs all its affections, that all
the remaining moments of my life, may be
entirely confecrated to your love.

Spiritual Communion by way of Viaticum.

*H Earken to your good Angel who invites
you to eat this bread of life, and fays to
you as to Elias.*

Rife and eat, for you have ftill à great
way to go.

*Reprefent to your felf that JESUS CHRIST,
attended by the Bleffed Virgin, your good
Angel and Patrons, enters your chamber to
adminifter to you his Sacred body with his
own Divine hands as he did to his Apoftles
at his laft fupper, and that he fays to you.*

Take and eat, this is my body which was
deliver'd to death for to give you life.

Having ador'd it with all your heart fay.

O my God! fince you have faid that he
who eats you, shall live eternally, and not
die, grant me the grace that by the reception
of your Sacred body, I may no more live,
but in you, by you, and for you; and that

leaving this mortal life, I may by the ſtrength
and vertue of this Divine Bread, attain in
heaven to the union and viſion of your Divine
Majeſty.

Ah! whence is this happineſs to me, that
my God comes to viſit me?

Lord I am not worthy that you should enter my ſoul, ſay only the word, and it ſhall
be cured.

*Having received him, entertain your ſelf
amourouſly with him, make all your ſenſes
and powers appear in his preſence, to offer
him the oath of fidelity. Renew the promiſes
you have made him : conjure him to leave
no more, and ſay with the Pilgrims of Emaus.*

Stay with me Lord, for it is late, the Evening of my life is come,

And with Holy Simeon.

Lord now diſmiſs my ſoul in peace ſince,
It has ſeen your ſalvation.

And with David.

Tho' I walk in the midſt of the shades of
death I will not fear any harm becauſe you
are with me.

O my God ! put your ſelf as à ſeal upon
my heart, that all earthly things may be ſhut
out of it.

Unite your Communion to that which this Divine Saviour made before his death, to all those that the Blessed Virgin and the Saints have made, and also to all those which shall be made even to the end of the world, to supply for your defects in receiving.

Thank your God for this particular favour, and for all those he has thereby so liberally bestow'd upon you. Invite all creatures to bless him for it, praise and thank him with them, reciting for that effect. Laudate Dominum omnes gentes, &c. *Or the canticle* Benedicite omnia opera, &c.

II. POINT.

SPIRITUAL EXTREME UNCTION.

I Magin that JESUS CHRIST *accompany'd as before, enters your chamber bringing the Sacred oil compos'd of his precious blood, which he intends himself to administer to you.*

In receiving them make these acts of contrition for the sins committed by each of your senses.

AT THE EYES.

1. O JESUS, my Saviour and my God! I most humbly beg pardon for all the sins I have committed by so many irregular looks, and vain tears: and to efface them, apply to me the merit of the amourous regards with which

on the Croſs you beheld your crucifiers, and the tears you ſhed for my ſalvation. .

AT THE EARS.

2. PArdon me alſo' the ſins I have committed by delighting to ,hearken to ſo many bad diſcourſes : and to ſatisfy for them, apply to me the merit of the patience, and humility with which your heard ſo many blaſphemies, injuries, and calumnies utter'd againſt you. -

AT THE NOSTRILS.

3. I Alſo moſt humbly beg pardon my God, for having too much ſought and taken delight in perfumes, and ſweet ſmells, and been too nice in ſhunning ill ones : to ſatisfy for theſe faults apply to me the merit of the ſtench you did ſupport in the ſtable, and on Mount Calvary.

AT THE MOUTH.

4. O My Saviour JESUS CHRIST, pardon me the infinite number of ſins I have committed by words and diſorderly eating or drinking : efface them I beſeech you, by applying to me the merit of your Divine Prayers, Preachings, and Holy faſts.

AT THE HANDS.

5. PArdon me my Divine JESUS, the many unprofitable, and ill actions that I have done,

together with my frequent feeking of what was foft and delightfull to touch : for which effect apply to me I befeech you, the merit of the Holy actions, and Divine Miracles you wrought with your Sacred hands, which were nail'd to the hard wood of the Crofs.

At the Feet.

6. O My God! from the bottom of my heart I befeech you to pardon me all my uielefs or ill fteps ; applying to me in fatisfaction for thofe faults, the merit of the Sacred fteps you trod bare foot with fo much pain and labour for the falvation of men, efpecially when you carry'd your Crofs.

After the extreme-unction make the following Acts in spirit of penance.

1. O My God! to fatisfy your juftice as much as I can, and make you an honorable amends of my whole being, I freely accept of death, and rejoice that my foul is to be feparated from my body in punishment of the fins it has committed , by rather following its irregular inclinations than your Holy will.

2. I am glad alfo that this body to punish its pride and ambition , is to be hid in the earth and trod under foot.

3. And for the inordinate love I have borne

it, and the too great care I have had to give
it eafe and pleafure, I rejoice it is to return
to rottennefs and be the food of worms.

4. I freely confent to the being deprived and
feparated from creatures, fince I have but too
much affected, and even abus'd them.

5. And for my forgetfulnefs of you my God,
during my life, I accept of being forgotten by
others after my death.

6. I likewife accept and offer you the priva-
tion of the ufe of my fenfes, becaufe I have fo
often ufed them to offend you.

7. And in punishment of my having fo often
vainly fought to pleafe creatures, I am content to be to them, by death, an object of
hatred and horrour.

THE APPROACHES OF DEATH.

*H Earken to your good Angel who fays to
you as to the Virgins of the Gofpel.*

Behold the fpoufe cometh, go then forth
to meet him.

*Preparing your felf for his coming with
the burning lamp of charity in your hand;
fay with David.*

I rejoice in the things that have been told
me : we shall go to the houfe of our Lord.

O Lord! God of vertues, how amiable are
your Tabernacles, my foul faints with wishing
for them.

My foul thirfts after God, the fountain of life! when shall I come and appear before his face?

As the thirfty Hart defires cooling ftreams: fo, my God! do's my foul defire you.

I defire to be deliver'd from this body, and to be with JESUS CHRIST.

Union with JESUS CHRIST dying.

O My Divine JESUS! grant me the grace to let my dolours be united with yours, my Agony, and my death be fanctify'd by yours, and that I may participate of the Sacred difpofitions of your Holy foul at the laft moment of your life, to which I unite my felf with all my heart, to fupply for thofe I want; and abandoning my felf to you, for to fuffer for your love as much of the pangs of death as you shall pleafe, I difavow all the imperfections that the pain may make me commit.

Have recourfe to the Bleffed Virgin and the Saints.

O Holy Virgin, Mother of my God, refuge of finners! be now my Advocate, and let me feel your power with the moft Bleffed Trinity.

O MARY, Mother of grace, Mother of mercy! receive me at the hour of death and defend me from the enemy.

O shew your felf à Mother! and obtain that he who for our falvation would be your Son and be born of you, receive us alfo by you.

O all yee Bleffed Angels and Saints of hea-ven, intercede now for my foul, and fuccour me in this extremity, that I may gain the victory over my enemies.

Great S. Jofeph, and my Holy protectors affift me.

Bleffed S. Michaël, fight for me.

Glorious Angel, my dear Guardian, defend me from the Ambufcade of my enemies, and forfake me not in this laft paffage.

Eternal Father, look on the face of your dear Son JESUS CHRIST, who has shed his blood for my falvation.

Have mercy on me according to the great-nefs of your mercies, and forgive me my fins for the glory of your name.

Enter not, my God, into Judgment with me, for none living can Juftify themfelves in your prefence.

My Divine JESUS! put your paffion, Crofs, and death, between your Judgment and my foul.

O God! my lot is in your hands, fave me I befeech you.

Lord I have hop'd in you, let me not be confounded for ever.

Act of Adoration to the most Blessed Trinity.

O Moft Holy, and undivided Trinity! I adore you with all my heart, and now unite my felf for eternity, to all the adorations and praifes, that the moft Holy Humanity of my Saviour J. C. that his moft Holy Mother, and that all the Saints and Angels, renders, and will eternally render you in heaven : I offer you all the Sacrifices, of that moft Holy Humanity, which are now offer'd, and will be offer'd you till the day of Judgment upon our Altars, in fatisfaction for my fins, and thanksgiving for all your Divine benefits.

CONCLUSION OF THIS EXERCISE.

ACT OF ABANDONMENT.

O My God! I abandon my felf totally and without referve to your Divine Judgments on my foul; I freely fubmit unto them, I adore and reverence them now, and for eternity, as moft Juft and equitable.

SPIRITUAL EXPIRATION.

Holding the Crucifix in your hand fay.

BEhold O my God, my Creator, and Redeemer! I come to you, becaufe you have call'd me, receive me into the bofom of your mercy.

Then amouroufly kiffing the wounds of your Crucifix, pronounce the Sacred names of JESUS and MARY, at each of them : and having said thefe laft words of your Saviour, into your hands my God I commend my fpirit, expire in the Sacred wound of your Saviours fide ; chufe it for your grave and hide your felf in his Divine heart.

After this exercife we ought to look on our felves as perfons dead to the world and to our felves, faying often with S. Paul, I live, but now not I, but JESUS CHRIST who lives in me ; my life is hidden with JESUS CHRIST in God.

❊❊❊❊❊❊❊❊❊❊❊❊❊❊❊

A PRAYER
When you go abroad.

MY Saviour I offer you the defigne of my going out, and defire it may be for your glory. Grant that I may feek you in all things, and find you in à whole eternity.

A PRAYER
When you make à vifit.

I Adore you my Saviour JESUS, who came from heaven to converfe with men : and I dedicate to you this vifit in honour of yours. Give

me

me à share of your charity and fincerity, preferve me from all that may difpleafe you, or
uncharitably offend my neighbour and permit
me not to confent to any fin.

A PRAYER
When you receive à vifit.

MY God, grant me the grace to receive
thefe vifitors rather according to the quality
of Chriftians than of that they hold in the
world, give me the fincere charity that you
command me to have for them. Keep me from
vain, and detracting difcourfes, and give me
the occafion of faying fomething which may
honour you and infpire your love.

A PRAYER
To be faid at the beginning or in time
of lafting actions.

ETernal love and charity, my God and my
all; I do this not by hazard or cuftom, nor
upon my own account, or for any others, but
for your fake, and to pleafe you by doing
your will; help O God the Father my memory, God the Son my underftanding, God
the Holy Ghoft my will, that I may remember, underftand, love, and execute your will
to your glory, the benefit and falvation of my
foul and others: MARY Mother of mercy
. M

protect me , my Guardian Angel help, conduct, and preferve me. Amen.

A PRAYER

To renew ones Baptifm.

MY Sovereign Lord and my God who was
mercifully pleas'd to let me enter into the bofom of your Church at the moment that I receiv'd Holy Baptifm, I now prefent my felf
at the feet of your Majefty to thank you for
it, and do moft humbly befeech you to accept
of the will I have to acknowledge this benefit
all the days of my life. I am forry I had not
capacity enough to praife and love you from
the moment of my Baptifm, but fince it was
an order of your Divine conduct on my foul,
I adore it, and defire this day to repair what
I did not do on the firft day of my Chriftian
life. I renew then in the prefence of heaven
and earth, my profeffion of faith, and proteft
that I will live and die in the Roman Catholick Religion. I renew the proteftation that I
made to renounce the devil and all his pomps.
I renew my obligations to conferve my body
in all purity, of which the Holy water ferv'd
me for à fymbol. I renew my promifes of regulating my life fo well that it may be an
example of all vertues. In à word, I again
make à proteftation to love you, ferve you,
and honour you, with more faith, more pu-

fity, and love than I have hithertodone. I
befeech you dear Lord, to give me ftrength
to execute what I purpofe, and to perfevere
in the exercife of the Catholick faith, to the
laft breath of my life. Amen.

A From of renewing the obligations of the Sacrament of Confirmation.

MY Lord God, how prodigious is the excefs of thy mercy, who not difcourag'd by
the ingratitude of men, pardon'ft them thofe
failings and fins, which they commit even
againft the Sacraments, the Sacred pledges of
thy love! I moft humbly beg pardon for the
unworthinefs I brought to the Sacrament of
Confirmation, for approaching to it without
being fully inftructed in its excellency, or
fill'd with a Holy zeal, and defire of living
all my days according to its fpirit and fanctity.

Proftrate therefore before thee, I here acknowledge I have convers'd amongft Chriftians
and thy children, without due veneration for
the Sacred Maxims of thy Gofpel; nay I
fear there has fcarce been any company, wherein I have been engag'd, or vifit I have made, wherein I have not fallen much beneath
the duty of a Chriftian, or done fomething
unworthy of that profeffion.

But now my God, I here purpofe and refolve to make it my endeavour for the future

to live as à good and faithfull Chriſtian, and being fortify'd by thy Holy grace, to appear as à ſoldier of JESUS CHRIST.

For this end I beg of thee à continual ſupport of thy grace, that the world, company, or cuſtom, may be never able to corrupt me by their pernicious maxims, that I may have ſtrength to reſiſt all ſhame and fear, which have ſo often hinder'd me from ſpeaking, and acting couragiouſly in my duty. Grant me alſo grace my God, that I may ſuffer in humility and ſilence, all the contradictions, affronts, and calumnies I ſhall meet with. And this one thing more I ask that I may no longer ſeek peace, and reſt in the things of this world, but in thy love only, and the vigorous practiſe of my duty, as may moſt contribute to thy honour.

When any communicates in your preſence, ſay.

JESUS Son of David have compaſſion on me.

My God have mercy on me poor ſinner, and give me tho taſt of thy banquet that my ſoul may be refreſh'd.

Dear Lord when ſhall I drink of thoſe fountains, which thy love has open'd for my comfort and relief.

Come O my Jesus! my heart expects you, my foul has an infatiable hunger of you.

O my Jesus! come to my heart, and build there à dwelling fit for your felf.

Dear Lord I own my felf unworthy, yet ftill I defire.

Precious body of my Saviour, fanctify all my members.

Moft Holy foul of my Lord Jesus, convert mine, and fill it with your love.

Dear Lord, my heart's already yours in defire, come then and poffefs it.

When not being at Mafs, you hear it toll SANCTUS, fay.

H Oly, Holy, Holy, is the Lord God of Hofts! how great is the diftance of his infinite Majefty from us poor worms below, heaven and earth are full of thy glory, grant Lord that our hearts may be alfo full of it, let heaven and earth blefs him that comes in the name of our Lord, 't is our gracious Lord himfelf who is coming, tho' after an invifible manner, Bleffed be his name.

When it tolls the firft Elevation.

I Adore you from the very bottom of my foul, O my Lord and Sovereign Redeemer! true and only Son of God, I adore your Divinity, and Sacred Humanity which I believe to be in the Hoſt now offer'd. I conſecrate to your honour and glory, my body, ſoul, life, and all that I am , proteſting that you are my ſalvation, and that I hope it from you alone, my good JESUS who has vouchſafed to die for me, have mercy on me.

When it tolls the ſecond Elevation.

ETernal Father, I offer you the Sacred blood of your Son, moſt humbly begging that the vertue of it may be apply'd for my ſalvation and that of all the faithfull. My Divine Saviour, let fall à drop of that ineffable blood which I actually adore, upon my ungrateful ſoul that it may beſoften'd, and return to you as to its center. Apply I beſeech you, your death to my life to vivify it, your fleſh to my ſoul to nouriſh and give it life , your vertue to my infirmity to fortify it, your grace to my faults to pardon them; your mercy to my miſeries to remedy them; your light to my darkneſs to diſperſe it, and enlighten me , your glory to my baſeneſs , to raiſe me and make me happy. Amen.

Aspirations upon all occuring objects.

In towns you will meet with people who go, come, fell, buy, work, each according to his vocation, at the fight of which, fay.

AH my God! that I took as much pains to gain heaven, as thefe people take for the perishable goods of this life!

Seeing à fine houfe.

O! in heaven there will be much finer pa-laces, and in them we shall live eternally, if we lead à Holy life in this world.

At the fight of à door or gate.

Mother of my JESUS, you are the gate of heaven, ah! open to my prayers the moft beautiful gate of the temple of God, and give me an entrance into that Bleffed aboad of eternity.

Of à Window,

Death enters our fouls by the windows which are our eyes. Be shut then my eyes to all the vanities of the earth, and all the deceitfull objects which feduces our reafon,

Of à River,

Ah! my life glides away like thefe waters, my days rolls like thefe waves.

Of à Bridge.

Ah! the bridge to à happy eternity is à good death, grant me then my God, the grace to lead à Holy life that I may attain to that happiness.

Of à tree loaden with fruit.

O that I was as well charg'd with merits! I am à barren tree good for nothing but to be caft into hell fire.

Of à rock.

I am harder than this rock, shall not your grace my God be able to foften the hardnefs of my heart.

Of à Fountain.

O JESÚS! Fountain of living water; when fhall I have that true thirft of Juftice, and figh only after heavenly goods? Purify my foul, water it with your graces.

Of à Garden well cultivated.

O that my foul were as perfectly cultivated as this garden! that it were as well adorn'd with vertues, as I fee excellent plants in this lovely place,

Of à Flower.

Here is the true image of the vanities of

this life. To day this flower is fresh and beautiful , and to morrow it will be faded and cast on the dunghill.

Of the Heavens.

There is my own country, what do I here? Why do I not elevate my thoughts and desires to the place where I hope to dwell for an eternity.

Of the Sun.

O Jesus! sun of Justice, illuminate me with the light of your grace.

The fool changes like the moon , now he takes à good design , and presently after he leaves it, O how foolish then am I.

When you are cold.

O if I felt the extreme coldness of my indevotions! what tears would they draw from me.

When incommoded with heat.

And what is this in comparison of the burning heats that are suffer'd in Purgatory?

When you smell à sweet smell.

O how much sweeter is the odour of virtue! draw me after you Lord , and we will follow you in the odour of your perfumes.

When you hear à concert of musick.

There will be much more ravishing musick in heaven.

When you see à person well dress'd.

O Vanity! of vanities, wilt thou always reign in the world? O my Saviour JESUS! give me à horror of all that the world so much esteems, and à love for all you have lov'd, and the world abhorrs so much.

If you see à coach full of people say
with David.

THese in coaches, and these on horses but we in the name of the Lord our God will invocate &c.

This their glory and their pleasure to be drawn by beasts, but all our glory O my Soul, and all our greatest satisfaction, ought to be only in going to God by the way of humiliations and sufferings.

Thus like à spiritual Bee you will draw
the honey of devotion from all objects, and
even turn the sins of others into good for
your self.

Passing by the Blessed Sacrament say kneeling.

My God I adore your Divine heart, and beg you to take possession of my poor miserable one.

At the sight of à Crucifix say to your self.

What God upon à Crosss, and shall I seek my ease?

O dear JESUS! grant I may so love, and suffer for you in my life, that you may have mercy on me at my death, I beg it by your Agony, and those bitter distresses of your heart at that passage.

Passing by our Ladys Altars and Pictures say.

Mother of God remember me.

But first make this Contract with our Lady.

O Mother of God, and my most dear Mother, by the heart of JESUS I beg you each time I shall say *Mater Dei memento mei*, to adore then for me that divine heart of your Divine Son, to offer my unworthy one unto him, begging pardon for all that's amiss in it, telling that God of love how much it desires perfectly to love him; and obtain me by your powerful intercession, à love that may consume in it all human loves and affections, and that he may replenish it to the full extent of its small capacity, and daily make it more and more capable of those heavenly flames : this dear Lady, I beg by the heart of JESUS, to

which I'm sure you can refuse nothing, and
by which I know you cannot be rejected;
O shew then your self à Mother, and comply
with the desire of your poor unworthy child,
obtain me à perfect love, and I'll desire no
more.

Renew this once à week.

✿✿✿✿✿✿✿✿✿✿✿✿✿✿✿✿✿

A Prayer proper for before and after
Sermons, Spiritual Lectures
and Catechisms, &c.

IMprint O Lord I beseech thee thy maxims
and rules of thy Gospel deep in my heart,
that whilst I profess my self à Christian, I may
not live like à heathen, for what will it profit
me to know thy will, and do it not, to hear
thy law and keep it not, this would be only
to turn the food of life into poison, and make
it, being the way to happiness be the encrease
of my damnation, deliver me O God from
this evil, and so perfectly at present possess
my heart, that my rebellious appetites being
overrul'd by thy grace, I may henceforth live
in the denial of my self, and like thy true
servant only hear and follow thee,

A Prayer before Holy Mass.

ALmighty and everlafting God, I prefume to appear before your infinite Majefty tho' moft unworthy, that I may pay you due honours by JESUS CHRIST your only Son. I am nothing in your fight, nor can do nothing of my felf, but by my Saviour who offers himfelf for me, I come to adore, blefs, and praife you. Amen.

A Prayer to obtain the grace of making à good Confeſſion.

LOrd fince you have promis'd us the pardon of our fins when we fincerely confefs them, give me your light to know them, your humility to accufe my felf of them, your love to have à true contrition for them, and your grace to avoid them for the future.

A Prayer before examen.

O My God! you fee the bottom of my heart, difcover to me all that has pafs'd therein contrary to your Holy will, let me know my pride, my remifsnefs, my irreverences, the lightnefs of my thoughts and words, and infine all that has difpleas'd you in me.

Act of Contrition.

O Moft infinitely amiable God! how unhappy am I in having fo much offended you. I am

confounded that I grieve no more for it, but
my God regard not my hardness, but the
excefs of grief with which the heart of JESUS
was feiz'd for me on the Crofs. I unite my
felf to his ardent love, and the extreme affliction his foul was plung'd in, feeing the injuries I have done you. Wash me in his tears,
and in his precious blood. I deteft my fins
which have caus'd his death, and purpofe
with your grace to make it my bufinefs to
avoid them for the future.

A Prayer after Confeffion.

I Return you moft humble thanks, O my God!
for the mercy you have shewn me in letting
me confefs my fins and receive abfolution of
them. I wish my contrition might equal that
of David, S. Mary Magdalen, S. Peter, and
all other Holy Penitents, and that I could
melt into tears to wash away perfectly all the
fpots of my foul. But I am like a dry flick,
and all my recourfe is to confide in my Saviour who has wept for me. Look my God,
on his grief upon the Crofs, and for the love
of him, excufe what has been wanting to my
confeffion, and give me the grace never to
offend you more, but to love you fincerely
all the days of my life. Amen.

A short Prayer to offer any action.

G Good JESUS! I offer you this action in
honour of the actions you did in the world.

Another.

O my JESUS! nothing for me, but all for
you, all purely for your glory and love.

A Prayer to be said when the clock strikes.

O my God! grant me the grace to return
each hour to your Divine presence. I acknowledge you for my God. I adore you, and give
you my heart. Preserve me from all sin, and
conserve me always in your Holy fear and love.

CHRISTIAN MAXIMS.

I.
That we are not created for this life, but
for heaven.

I I.
That the most important affair which we
have in this life, is our salvation.

I I I.
That salvation is not obtain'd without pains
and labour.

I V.
That our chiefest care in this life must be
to please God and live in his grace.

(192)

V.

That we cannot be in the grace of God without having a constant resolution never to offend him upon any score.

VI.

That sin is the greatest evil which can befall a man.

VII.

That the worst of all misfortunes, is to die in mortal sin.

VIII.

That this misfortune happens to many, and to those who think not of it.

IX.

That we must think frequently on death, Jugdment, and Eternity.

X.

That we must serve God for himself, and by love.

XI.

That we must have a rule of our actions, and that this rule ought to be the law of God, the example and doctrine of JESUS CHRIST; and not the world nor the example of others, nor custom.

XII.

That the world is deceiv'd in all its Judgments and maxims.

XIII.

That to be united only to God, we must contemn earthly things.

ADVERTISMENTS.

ADVERTISEMENTS

For young people Juſt entering into the world.

I. ADVERTISEMENT.

THat the time of iſſuing out of youth and entering into the world, is the moſt dangerous of all our life, and many are shipwrack'd therein.

II.

That the chief care of young people who enter into the world, ought to be to conſerve the ſentiments, and pra&ctiſes of piety, which they have obſerv'd in their youth.

III.

That young people muſt carefully fly wicked company, and particularly that of young vicious perſons of their profeſſion.

IV.

That they muſt ſpeedily apply themſelves to ſome labour, which may employ their time and make them avoid idleneſs, which is then moſt dangerous and more than at any other time.

V.

That they muſt avoid at that time irreſolution concerning the ſtate they ought to chuſe, and after the choiſe, not eaſily, nor without great reaſon change.

N

V I.

That young people ought to forefee the dangers, and obligations of their profeſſion, acquit themſelves of their obligations, and live virtuouſly in their profeſſion, according to God.

V I I.

That they muſt accuſtom themſelves betimes, not to be aſham'd of virtue, nor of performing the actions thereof.

V I I I.

That they muſt have a care to embrace a ſolid and real vertue, and not an apparent and deceitful piety.

I X.

That young perſons ought to fix themſelves more and more in the ſolid ſentiments of faith and religion.

That they muſt be ſtrongly ſettl'd in the aforeſaid Chriſtian maxims oppoſite to thoſe of the world.

To conclude, remember Ladies, that life paſſes, death advances, eternity approaches, life is but a moment, and on this moment depends eternity. O moment! O eternity, let us at leaſt employ this moment to ſerve our Creator, who deſerves an eternity of ſervice. Let us conſecrate our ſelves during this mortal life to that Adorable goodneſs, who gives

himfelf fully to us for all eternity. Let nothing
be able to feparate us from his fervice. *Who
shall feparate us from the charity of* Jesus
Christ? Says the Divine Apoftle. O God!
permit it not, but caufe by thy Divine bounty, that our hearts be infeparabily united unto
thee ; and that performing thy will in all
things, we may love thee perfeverantly in this
life, to love, adore, and blefs thee for ever
in heaven, where thou liveft, and reigneft
world without end. Amen.

*A Monthly review, firft Meditation, the
fubject of which is taken out of the
Parable of the barren fig tree.*

I. POINT.

COnfider 1. with what care God has hitherto
all along cultivated us, to make us bring forth
fruit. We came into the world not only as à
barren tree, but alfo as à tree fpoil'd, blafted
originally by fin, and fit for nothing but to
be hew'n down and caft into hell fire, God
thro' his fingular mercy has preferably to fo
many others, tranfplanted us, as one may
fay, into his Church by making us Chriftians,
and plac'd you if not in religion, at leaft in
à religious houfe, in which the due care of

thofe to whom he has confided your educa-
tion will lead you ftep by ftep, in the eafie
yet advantagious practifes of true virtue, and
help you to lay à fure foundation for à Holy
and happy life. With what comfort then ought
you to enjoy this fo valuable à blefling? How
thankful should you be to God for it, and
how attentive to produce the fruit he expects
from you? Have you hitherto been fo, at leaft
this laft month? What have you produc'd?
And what will you endeavour?

II. POINT.

COnfider 2ly. that by the fruit which God
requires of us, is not meant fome certain barren practifes of devotion, and certain out-
fides of virtue which commonly ferve but to
amufe imperfect perfons, who with all thefe
pretended good works, pafs their whole life
in lukewarmnefs, without mending one fingle
fault; bu the fruits God would have from us,
are the effects of à true love for him, and à
perfect charity towards our neighbour; fruits
a folid piety produces; that is to fay, à horrour of the fmalleft fins, an infatiable hunger
after Juftice, à conftant, and univerfal mortification, à profound humility, and à great
exactnefs in all the duties of our ftate and
condition, à mighty averfion for every thing
our Saviour hates, and à particular efteem for

all he loves, à compleat victory over paffions, and an entire reformation of our lives and manners, this in general to all : but for you in particular, thefe fruits may be reduc'd to what your rule requires of you; that is devotion in general and particular as there defin'd, Modefty, à fweet and patient meeknefs, Humility, purity of body and mind, Obedience and Tractability, Charity, good example, diligence, and punctual obfervance of your rules fitted for your prefent ftate, as the foundation of your future happinefs, both in time and eternity ; this is the fruit God exacts of you ; what have you produc'd in this laft month ? What will you endeavour in the next?

III. P o i n t.

COnfider 3ly. the danger we run by leading an unfruitful life, and how much we ought to dread, drawing down upon us the vengeance of God, and that terrible fentence of reprobation which was given againft the barren tree. Think how many graces you have depriv'd your felf of, and how many you have loft : Ah fear to be depriv'd for ever of thofe great fuccours which you have made ineffectual ! For inward recollection being once loft, the foul will expofe, or let it felf loofe indifferently to all forts of objects, it will become as it were à prey to all paffions, God will no more move you, not enter into the bottom of your heart, wholsome saving advices will make no more impreffion on you, the fource and fountain of grace will be dry'd up. And what shall become of a foul in this fad and wretched condition? Yet this may be expected by thofe barren fouls that bear no fruit.

Alas Lord! enter not into Judgment with thy fervant, becaufe none can appear innocent in your fight : I own that I have hitherto been not only a barren and unfruitful tree but a corrupted one. That I have unprofitably taken up a place in a fruitful field, and by confequence, am only fit to be hew'n down and caft into the fire. *But have patience with me*, Not for a year, but for a day, and I hope with the help of your grace to make fo good ufe of this day, that I shall render your care no longer ineffectual.

II. MEDITATION.

Of the good ufe of time.

I. POINT.

COnfider 1. there is nothing more precious than time : all its moments are worth an eternity : an everlafting happinefs, the glory of the bleft, the price of the blood of JESUS, all this is but the recompenfe of our making good

ufe of time. Time is fo precious à thing that
all the honour , and all the wealth of the
world are not worth fo much as one of its
moments; and altho' we should have employ'd
but one moment in acquiring all the riches
of the world , if we have not got fomething
better in the fight of God who makes à right
Judgment of all things, it is to have mifpent
our time ; and there is not à damn'd foul
which would not give all the kingsdoms, and
wealth of the world, if in his power, for one
moment of the time he has loft in trifles, and
which we our felves , as he did , do daily
lofe for toys and vanities. Let us conceive if
poffible, what à grace is, and how much the
enjoyment of God is worth : this grace, and
this God are the price of time which is given
us for no other end , but to encreafe every
moment more and more in grace , to merit
thereby the poffeffion of God ; and we may
truly fay that in each moment which we have
not employ'd for God , we have loft more than
the whole world is worth. What the Saints
in heaven can never do by the moft perfect
acts of the greateft virtues ; to wit to merit
à new degree of glory; that I can do every
moment of the day by one fingle act of the
love of God. What the reprobate can never
do by their tears, forrows, and all the moft
dreadfull punishment , to wit to affwage the

wrath of God, and obtain pardon for their crimes; that I can do at any time by one figh, by one tear, for by one fingle act of contrition I can obtain pardon of all my fins.

II. POINT.

COnfider 2ly. à happy or an unhappy eternity, depends upon the good, or ill ufe we make of time; and yet there are people who know not what to do with it, who amufe, and bufie themfelves about trifles to pafs away the time : you know not what to do with it? Ah! have you never then offended God? Do you not know how to lament it ? Have you no obligations to him ? And ought you not to pay him fome homage ? All eternity feems not long enough to the Saints to love him, to blefs, honour, and thank him, and yet one half day, nay one half hour, feems perhaps too long for you to fpend fo. But tho' the generality are fo unhappy as this, yet you can not be of the number, having your duties chalk'd out by your rules, and times appointed for them, fo that you have but to pray, read, write, work, and innocently recreate, in the appointed times and places, with an intention, and defire to pleafe God thereby, and your time is very well fpent, for à happy eternity. But if befides all this you happen to have fome time at your free difpofal, be not so childish as to trifle it away; let the devotion of the day, or your own particular devotion, pioufly employ you, for time is short, becaufe it laft's but ones life, you have perhaps already fpent more than half yours, and what ufe have you made of it? At leaft how have you fpent this laft month? It is but time loft to have done what you ought not to do, and not to have done what you were oblig'd to. Lament your paft failings, fee how you may amend, and beg grace for the fame. ,

III, P O I N T.

COnfider 3ly. that the lofs of time is an irreparable lofs : for let men do all they can, they will never be able , to recover one loft moment. 'Tis certain that all the moments of our life are counted, the number is determin'd, and decreafes every minute : an hour ago we had more time to live , and confequently to labour in the bufinefs of our falvation, and within an hour we shall have yet lefs. Tho' hereafter we lofe not one moment more of the remainder of our time ; yet that time already loft will never be retriv'd. And all the moments of our life, which have been ill employ'd are irrevocably loft : the well employing of our time to come may likely draw us out of the danger into which we had before precipitaded our felves by mifpending our time paſt, but it cannot reſtore the time we have loſt, nor prevent our loſing by that loſs, all the graces which God deſign'd us, and all the good which in that time we might have done. Let us here conſider what uſe we have made of our time paſt; it is gone, and if it be loſt, how great alas is our loſs? And what means is their left to repair it? What fair days, what good hours, and what moments in thoſe days have we loſt? Thoſe that ſpend their time well, never think it tedious; and had we done ſo, what a comfort would it be to us? But what regret muſt we have for having loſt all this time, and ſo been unfruitful trees. Let us at leaſt make an advantage of the remainder of our time by employing it in what we know God requires of us, in our preſent ſtate and condition; for a time will come when we can reap no more benefit by time, becauſe it will be ſwallow'd up in eternity. Let us then make a good uſe of the little time we have yet to come, and for the future not loſe an other moment.

III. MEDITATION.

Of the fruits of repentance.

I. POINT.

COnſider 1. that there is no way to get to heaven but by mortification and repenance;

JESUS CHRIST has shew'd us no other, and
the Saints themfelves who in their Mothers
womb were confirm'd in grace, went no other
way. It is an errour to believe that penance
is only neceffary for great finners; nor is it à
lefs miftake to imagine that mortification is à
virtue proper only for perfect fouls. If we are
finners, we are oblig'd to repent, to endeavour to foften Gods Juftice, and to obtain
pardon from his mercy for our crimes : if we
are fo happy as never to have loft our innocence, penance is not the lefs neceffary to
preferve that precious treafure : we may fin,
we have finn'd are the two powerful motives
to induce us to practife it. Can we reafonably
believe that penance is only proper for fuch
as are religious, and that mortificatious should
reign only in cloifters, fince all agree that in
the world people fin much oftner, and that
there is in it much more danger? Let them
but reflect that thofe religious perfons whom
they think indifpenfably oblig'd to the exercife of penance, did for the moft-part enter
religion with out lofing their innocence, and
yet that perfons who do not difown their having committed à great many fins, and who
are every moment in danger of committing
more, should go about to perfwade themfelves that mortification, and penance are not
things proper for them, is very ftrange and

wonderful. Altho' we had nothing but our own paſſions to tame and conquer, could we reaſonably hope to ſucceed without the exerciſe of penance? And who can with reaſon hope to work out his ſalvation without overcoming his paſſions? It is an article of faith, that none but ſuch as uſe violence to themſelves, ſhall enter heaven, and yet we pretend to get thither without mortification. The life of à man upon earth is à continual warfare; for the fleſh (as S. Paul ſays) has deſires contrary to thoſe of the ſpirit, and the ſpirit has deſires contrary to thoſe of the fleſh, and without the exerciſe of penance, what hope to overcome.

II. POINT.

Conſider 2ly. that by the fruits of penance is underſtood not only the mortification of the body. But principally, the ſubduing of the paſſions, and the reformation of manners: theſe are properly the fruits which God expects from our contrition and repentance; by theſe marks it may be known whether we make à good uſe of the Sacraments, truly grieve for our ſins, and are faithful managers of the grace which God hath given us. The practiſes of devotion, the frequent uſe of the Sacraments, and the exerciſe of good works, are powerful means to make men become perfect;

but fo long as with thefe powerful means they have ftill the fame paffions; are ftill equally proud, impatient, fretful, envious, uneafie, angry, unmortify'd, and full of felf love, can thefe pretended exercifes of piety be reckon'd upon, with any manner of reafon? The ufe of bodily mortification is an exercife of penance, but this penance muft bring forth fruit, and this fruit confifts in reparing the diforders of our paffion, and the irregularities of felf love. What fignifies it to confefs faults fo often, if we mend not one fault in à year of all we have confefs'd. 'Tis not enough to deteft ones fins, we muft alfo make à refolution never to commit any more of them ; but can this very refolution be fincere, if not accompany'd with à will to fly the leaft occafion of fin. Every one has fome thing to fuffer during this life, we find croffes every where, let us at leaft fuffer with patience, let us join our fufferings to thofe of Jesus Christ : we shall not fuffer the more by it, and our fufferings will not then be fruitlefs. The conftant exercife of mortification is alfo another fruit of penance, what vaft fruit might one not draw from it? There is nothing which may not furnish us with an occafion of contradicting our natural inclinations; there is no time nor place that is not proper to mortify our felves without being extravagant. O what advantage

may one who truly loves JESUS, make by
thefe little occafions! If one has à great mind
to look, or fpeak in fome certain circumftances, how profitable is it then to caft down
ones eyes, or hold ones peace? There's hardly
an hour of the day that affords not à fubject
of mortification; whether we fit, or ftand, or
kneel, we may ever find ways privately to
incommode our felves. But above all, let us
endeavour exactly to comply with the rules,
and orders of our ftate, for thofe are the moft
precious fruits of mortification : what have you
produc'd this laft month? What will you endeavour in the next?

III. P o i n t,

COnfider 3ly. there is yet another more neceffary fruit of penance, without which all
others will fignify but very little in order to
eternity, and this is the reformation of manners, and the overcoming our predominant
paffion. Let us obferve which of our paffions
has the chief fway over us, and the habit
which influences our actions; our moft ordi-
nary and familiar fin, and which is in fome
manner the fource of all the reft, the caufe
of all the falfe maxims we frame to our felves
in matters of confcience; we may be ftrangers
to all other vices, but our proper character
is to be taken from the prevailing paffion, the

paffion that Lords it over us. The fruit of a true converfion is to cut off the vice which reigns in us : to deteft with a pious horrour this imperious domineering paffion, to the end we may afterwards fight againft it continually, and without intermiffion. This victory alone will fecure us againft the ftrongeft temptation of the enemy : we eafily make war againft our other vices, but this is commonly fpar'd, and that is the reafon we reap but little fruit by our penance.

O My God! I am refolv'd to omit nothing that may make me lead à lefs barren life. I can do nothing without your grace, and with that, I can do all things; and fince you yet give me time to repent, permit me no longer to abufe this time, fince from this moment I am refolv'd to bring forth fruits worthy of re-pentance.

*A Confideration, or examen upon your Chrif-
tian duties towards God, your neighbour,
and your felf, and firft.*

TOWARDS GOD.

1. **A**Re you practically convinc'd that your
whole duty by creation, adoption, and the
folemn engagement of your baptifm, is not to
feek, in this life your private intereft and con-
tènt but to honour, praife, and ferve God;
and that all creatures ferve to your ufe only
upon that account, and to help you to difcharge your duty ? Can you by confequence
truly fay with David? *As the eyes of à handmaid are ever on her miftreffes hands to obey
the leaft fign of her will, fo my eyes are
attentive on God.*

2. How do's your mind and heart ferve
him? For thofe belong to God alone. What
fubmiffion do you pay to his infinite Sove-
reignty? To his power and dominion? What
efteem have you of his infinite numberlefs benefits, and gifts? What fenfe of your obligation to honour, and ferve him in, and by all
that you do and fuffer? What refpect do you
bear every where to his prefence? What confidence have you in his protection? How frequent acts of love do you pay to his goodnefs
and mercy.

3. How

3. How do your words ferve him? With what refpect, attention, love, fervour, do you pray to him? With what willingnefs, and tendernefs do you fpeack of him? With what frequency of an humble and loving recourfe to him, do you by interiour afpirations fpeak to him?

4. How do your works and employments ferve him? Do you with an equal fubmiffion accept of all the difpofitions of his providence? Do you refer all things to his glory? Do you chiefly feek to pleafe God by all your actions, performing what he employs you in the beft way you can? Are you eafily refign'd to what ever fuccefs his providence allows? For if not, your chief aim is not the performance of his will. Do you fuffer with content for his fake? And are you willing to have occafions of giving him that proof of your fubmiffive love? Do you grieve, and that readily and fenfibly, at what offends him in you or others?

5. Do you fatisfy his Juftice by penance? Do you make your firft recourfo to him in all difapointments, afflictions, bufinefs? Do you return your firft thanks to him in Joyful occafions? Do you offer him frequent volontary facrificces? Do you give due attention and obedience to his infpirations? Do you adore, and praife him in all forts of events?

O

II. Towards your Neighbour.

1. WHat do you generally imagine and consider in each of those you converse with? Do
you look on them as children of God, or
spouses of Christ, his substitutes, to whom he
will have you pay the good will and services
you owe him? As fellow travellers towards à
blissfull eternity, to. be shar'd and enjoy'd
without end? Or do you look on some, as the
objects of aversion, or sensual affection, of
contempt, or anger? Which of these so oppo-
site considerations guide your thoughts, or
your affections, words or actions, in regard
to them?

2. Survey your mind in order to your neighbour: is there no ill propension to Judge un-
kindly, or suspect harsly of any one? No se-
cret envy, jealousie, or bitterness, which leads
you to misinterpret their designs and intentions
in what they speak and do?

3. How stands your heart towards each?
If any aversion be harbour'd but against one,
in case you feed it, and oppose it not, you
will not remain long in the state of grace.
Saul saith Holy writ, look'd upon David with
an unkind eye, the malice of which improv'd
for forty years, and ended but with his reprobation. If yours be but à natural antipathy,
t'wil be no hurt, but à help to grace, in case

you look on it, as an humbling misery, pray
to be freed from it; speak and act in regard
of that person, as you would do had you a
natural kindness for her.

4. If any fond affection dwell in your heart :
't is à viper in your breast which may every
moment sting you to death : if you look on it
otherways, it will certainly be most hurtful,
and may be your ruin. To feel it tho' never
so violent, is no hurt to the soul, so you
think it to be à dangerous distemper and treat
it accordingly, by doing nothing to express,
or feed it ; and keeping watch that God be,
not turn'd out of your thoughts, or heart, to
place à creature in them; and that you never
cease to serve him alone, by slavery to another.

5. Observe your words concerning others.
Is here no harshness with à design to mortify ? No uncharitable jests, no pride, haugh-
tiness, and contempt? Do your words favour
any in their faults, or occasion them ? That's
the sin of scandal. Are you so unhappy as
ever to drop from your mouth à burning coal,
that shall kindle aversion or dislike in any
one towards another ?

6. Is it your weakness to be ever attentive
to what others say or do, and never to the
use you make of their words and actions, that
you may secure à virtuous one ? Do you as
much as you can encourage virtue in each,

lay paffions, breath eafe and confort to the
uneafy or afflicted?

III. Towards your self.

1. **A**Re your thoughts, defigns, labours,
fpent on the concerns of this life, or on thofe
of the next? That is, what do you geuerally
feek, is it to pleafe your humour and inclina-
tion or to pleafe and content God? That you
may not miftake, go thro' the actions of the
day, obferve what you feek, in, and by them..

2. All will perifh who do not penance fays
our Lord. How do you nourish or neglect interiour penance? How frequent are your acts
of contrition efpecially in Prayer? How affi-
duous an humble reflection on your frailties
and faults? Do you eafily find, and own your
felf faulty?

3. As to exteriour penance, do you by the
motive of it deprive your felf freely of fome
fatisfactions which tho' unneceffary, would be
agreeable to you? With what eafie fubmiffion
do you accept of thofe God fends you by
what ever fufferings, efpecially from humours
difagreeable to yours? Is it with willingnefs
and charitable peace? What labours and pains
do you embrace of choice, purely upon Gods
account, and to fatisfy for your faults?

4. As to neceffary diverfions, eafes, and fa-

tisfactions of life, do you use them with due
measure, without delivering up your heart to
them? With what referve, not to expofe your
mind or heart to dangerous engagements that
might clog their freedom and liberty?

5. What due care do you take that your
thoughts be profitably employ'd? As for the
different affections and inclinations of your
heart, what objects take them up, fuch as
fanctify, or fuch as fully it?

*See in what you are mofi faulty, and what
will be the befl remedy. And write down your
refolutions for the next month, which you
should often read, and beg grace for the performance of them,*

SALVE REGINA.

HAil to the Queen who reigns above,
Mother of clemency & love :
Hail thou our hope, life, fweetnefs; we
Eve's banifh'd children cry to thee.
We from this wretched vale of tears
Send fighs and groans unto thine ears;
O! then fweet Advocate, beftow
A pitying look on us below.
After this exile, let us fee
Our Blefled! J E S U S born of thee :
O Merciful! O pious maid!
O gracious Mary, lend thine aid,

℣. Pray for us, O Holy Mother of God!
℟. That we may be made worthy of the pro-miffes of CHRIST.

Let us Pray.

O Almighty & Eternal God, who didſt pre-pare the body & ſoul of the glorious Mary, Mother & Virgin, that by the cooperation of the Holy Ghoſt she might become a worthy habitation for thy Son : grant, that as we re-joice in her commemoration, ſo by her pious interceſſion , we may be deliver'd both from preſent evils, and everlaſting death, thro' the ſame JESUS CHRIST our Lord. Amen.

FINIS.

THE CONTENTS.

APPROBATION.

THis *Collection of Prayers and Devotions*
is very proper to form, and forward the hearts
of the *young Ladies and Gentlewomen*, for
whom its design'd in the *one only necessary*
practise of the *Presence*, and *Love* of Almighty
God. It's therefore I Licence it to be publish'd
for *Mr. DE MARCQ* Doctor of Divinity, and
Censor of Books in this University. Doway, at
the English Recollects this 5. of January 1712.

F. *FRANCIS KEARNY* Reader of Divinity.

APPROBATION.

I Have read by authority this Collection of
Prayers and Devotions, and find nothing contrary to faith and good manners.

F. *BRUNO CANTRILL* Reader of Divinity.

9 783741 166341